Third Morning Cloud

Edward Heath
SAILING
A Course of My Life

STEIN AND DAY/Publishers/New York

**To the crew of *Morning Cloud,* without whom nothing
could have been achieved, and to those who lost their lives,
Christopher Chadd, my godson, and Nigel Cummings.**

Front end papers:
Third *Morning Cloud* reaching off
Burnham with the spinnaker up.
Left to right: Duncan Kay,
Terry Leahy, Tubby Lee, self
Title page: Fourth *Morning Cloud*
on trials, June 1975

Most of the photographs in
this book are from the author's
private collection. We are
indebted to him for their use

First published in the United States of America, 1976
Copyright © 1975 by Edward Heath
and Sidgwick and Jackson Limited

Designed by Paul Watkins

Printed in Great Britain

Stein and Day/Publishers/
Scarborough House, Briarcliff Manor, N.Y. 10510

Library of Congress Cataloging in Publication Data

Heath, Edward.
    Sailing: a course of my life.

    1. Heath, Edward.   2. Sailing. I. Title.
DA591.H4A36   941.08'092'4 [B] 75-29912
ISBN 0-8128-1886-5

Contents

Morning Cloud gybing just before the finishing line at Hobart, Tasmania. Sammy Sampson and Jean Berger, the helmsmen, are on the foredeck

6

1 End of the Sydney-Hobart Race

31 December 1969

As we sailed up the River Derwent towards Hobart I could feel the tension growing. The wind, which had been some 25 to 30 knots across the deck as we came out of Storm Bay at the entrance to the river, had been steadily dropping. Now it was light and looked like dropping away altogether. Were we to be denied our victory so close to the line? It is the moment every racing sailor fears.

The tension was understandable. It was only at one o'clock that afternoon, as we were crossing Storm Bay, that my navigator heard on the local Tasmanian radio that if we were across the line by six o'clock that evening we would win the twenty-fifth Sydney–Hobart Race. Until then we had not thought we had a chance. According to the news very few boats were already in the dock. In fact only three big boats, including Sir Max Aitken's British boat *Crusade,* which had fought a running battle with Alan Bond's Australian boat *Apollo* all the way down the coast, were home. But three others were reported moving up-river, including the second boat for the British team, Arthur Slater's *Prospect of Whitby.* Now here we were, only a few hundred yards from the finishing line at the entrance to the dock, with the wind behind us, our light floater spinnaker up, and only the merest breeze.

I was at the helm myself, the other five members of the crew around me in the stern. I had told them that as we were in a winning position we had better freshen ourselves up after more than four days at sea and make ourselves look as seaman-like as possible. The quickest and easiest way of doing this was to put on our white and blue oilies, which the weather and summer heat made neither necessary nor bearable. But at least we would sail – or drift – into Hobart looking respectable.

As we moved slowly ahead I took a moment to glance to each side of us. The docks were crowded with people peering towards us. Behind them were rows and rows of cars stretching back up the hillsides. The sun shone on the clean, white buildings. I could see what was presumably the Committee boat waiting at what must be the finishing line itself. Even at that distance I could sense the excitement of the crowds.

The wind became lighter still and I realized that the boat was being gently headed towards the river bank to the south. All the time I was trying to counter this, easing her along so that we would still be able to hit the finishing line. I could feel the crew becoming more and more apprehensive, and when we were some 150 yards away from the Committee boat I realized that we would not be able to reach it without gybing. Reluctantly I gave the order, 'Prepare to gybe!' So strung up were the crew that the two helmsmen, who normally stood in the cockpit as the afterguard, leapt forward, to the astonishment of the foredeck hands, and ran to seize the spinnaker pole to gybe the boat. As one of the foredeck crew said afterwards: 'They had never been up there before and I don't suppose they will ever be up there again.'

I could almost hear the crowd draw in its breath as they watched

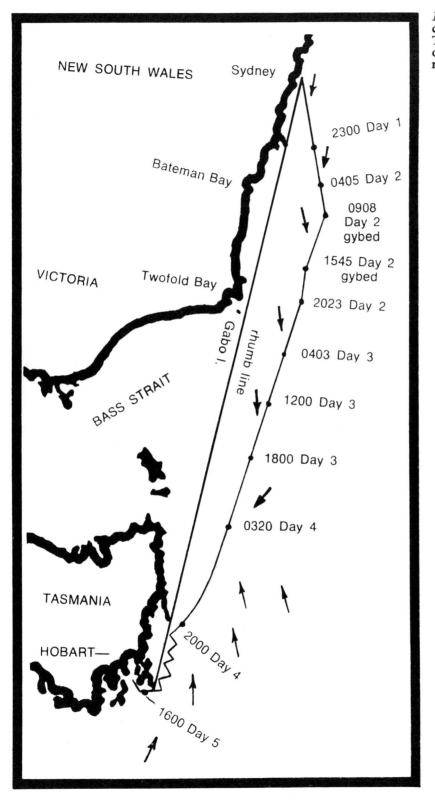

NEW SOUTH WALES   Sydney

2300 Day 1

Bateman Bay

0405 Day 2

0908
Day 2
gybed

VICTORIA   Twofold Bay

1545 Day 2
gybed

2023 Day 2

Gabo I.

rhumb line

0403 Day 3

1200 Day 3

BASS STRAIT

1800 Day 3

0320 Day 4

TASMANIA

HOBART—

2000 Day 4

1600 Day 5

Morning Cloud's course compared to the rhumb line. The Sydney-Hobart Race, one of the three great ocean-racing classics

us gybe so close to the finishing line. None of us would claim afterwards that it was the best gybe that we had ever done, or that it resembled in any way our normal drill, but it served its purpose which was all that mattered.

With the wind lightened still further I gently moved the tiller over and we continued our progress towards the line. It seemed to take an interminable time, but as we inched forward everything in view became clearer and clearer. We could see the tops of the masts of the boats already in. We could begin to see individual faces among the crowd; then we were coming up to the Committee boat. The excitement increased.

At last we found ourselves crossing the finishing line. And as we did so all bedlam broke loose. Every car within range was hooting its horn, the crowds cheered, and the sirens went. Everything happened so quickly. The launch came alongside to tow us into the dock. We dropped the spinnaker. The tension on the boat suddenly collapsed. We found ourselves laughing with joy. I had a lump in my throat. In almost the smallest boat of the lot we had won the Sydney-Hobart Race.

We tied up alongside the big boats already in. The British on *Crusade* burst into some familiar nautical songs appropriate to the occasion. The crowds surging along the dock seemed to enjoy their somewhat bawdy flavour. It is said that in his excitement a member of another British crew promptly climbed the mast of his boat, exposing his bottom as he went. That we never saw, for on *Morning Cloud* we were busy trying to realize that our victory was real. I took a glance around the boat to find that Owen Parker was already quietly getting the spinnaker sheets and guys off the deck and stowing sails, quite oblivious to the welcome which was about to descend upon us.

First to come on board was a representative of the local Tasmanian brewery bringing a large case of canned beer. We were – and still are – a dry boat, so this went down well. Cans were popping all over the place. Then we were invaded by the television cameras and the press photographers, all wanting pictures of different groupings at the same moment. By this time it had become rather a scrum on board.

Having got through all that and thinking I would relax in the cockpit with the rest of the crew for a few moments I found our third visitor had arrived. He was a tall, well-dressed young man who stood smartly in front of me and said: 'Sir, the Governor presents his compliments and is delighted you are able to stay with him at Government House. He has asked me to tell you that he is expecting you there for dinner tonight, quarter to eight for eight o'clock – black tie.' And with that request I knew that the British and all their traditions were still firmly ensconced in that far-away part of Australia. We really had come home!

After thanking him I pulled myself together and said: 'In that case I must find my baggage.' The Australians, with that helpful efficiency of which we had already had a great deal of experience, had collected all our baggage in Sydney and flown it, free of charge, down to Hobart. The Governor's A.D.C. had already discovered the shed on the dock where it had been stacked. He promptly led me along there only to find that of all the crews of the seventy-nine-strong fleet, mine was the only suitcase which had gone astray.

There was nothing for it but to go to Government House as I was. That night I dined there with the Governor, his family and friends, in whites with the dark blue *Morning Cloud* sailing sweater. It must be the first and probably the last time that a sailor home from the sea has dined there in such a garb.

Dinner over I rejoined the crew in their celebrations, now in the Yacht Club in Hobart. All of them appeared to be giving television interviews with what seemed reckless impunity. They were celebrating not only a sailing victory, they were celebrating a successful gambling operation. For unknown to me they had joined in the betting which had taken place on the race, and so confident were they of *Morning Cloud* that they had put their money on our own boat. They were busy spending the profits.

Eventually the parties broke up. It was a late night, or, rather, an early morning. But who could blame us? The Sydney–Hobart Race is one of the three great ocean-racing classics of the world – and some would say very often the toughest. After a long, fast spinnaker run we had come through an Antarctic gale. The first race, in 1945, had been won by John Illingworth, who was British. We were the first British to win it since, and we had done so our first time out. Whatever happened in the future, this was something no one could ever take away from us or from *Morning Cloud.*

A welcome can of beer was waiting for us when we arrived in the dock at Hobart. Left to right: Sammy Sampson, Jean Berger, Anthony Churchill, Owen Parker, self, Duncan Kay

2 How It All Began

What led us into the Sydney–Hobart Race? How did it all begin?

One weekend in the early summer of 1966 I was down at my home in Broadstairs on the Channel coast. The North Foreland lighthouse a mile or two out of the town is just about the eastern-most point of England. Looking out from the cliffs on any clear day we can see straight across to Calais and the coast of France. For most of the year we are used to the heavy Channel seas and with the three light-vessels on the gruesome Goodwin Sands always blinking to warn us, we know all about the perils of the sea. We have a jetty there to protect us from the Northerlies and the Easterlies. The bay protects us to the west and the south. There is a small harbour, but it is tidal and in most cases you cannot get a boat in or out unless it is within two hours either side of high tide.

Above the jetty, in a commanding position, stands Bleak House, or Fort House as it was known when Charles Dickens lived there. The novelist spent many of his holidays in the town and there is quite a rash of houses each with its plaque commemorating the books he wrote while staying there—*Bleak House, Nicholas Nickleby* and *David Copperfield*. The notable exception is a small but charming cottage in a street back from the promenade, which has beside its door a neat and beautifully lettered marble tablet which states quite simply: 'Charles Dickens did not live here.' It makes the point. 'A old-fashioned watering place' was how Charles Dickens described Broadstairs in his time, and it remains unspoilt to this day.

Broadstairs. Previous pages: In the early nineteenth century, from an original sketch by Master Hue and (this page) a photograph taken today from much the same spot. North Foreland one design class are now moored off the jetty at the far end of the bay where the fishing smacks used to tie up

I was born there and for most of my life there has been a home there to which I could always return. In two world wars my parents left to live near London, but afterwards our family lives resumed their normal routine. I went to school in Ramsgate nearby, and while I was at Oxford I went back there when term ended. After I became a Member of Parliament, and later a Minister, the number of weekends I could spend at home became fewer. Inevitably, after I became Leader of the Conservative Party in July 1965 I had even less time for my home life. Almost every weekend there was a function to attend or a speech to be made in some other part of the country. However, I was desperately trying to keep at least one day free at each weekend for some sort of recreation. I knew how stale one would get without it. After all, I had seen four Prime Ministers burn themselves out and I had no desire, if the time came, to follow their example.

My doctor and good friend, Brian Warren, had recently been getting rather firm about this. In January 1959 I had had a bad attack of hepatitis — jaundice, as I always knew it. This insidious and intensely boring disease demanded a régime of lemon juice one day, orange juice the next, barley water on the third, lime juice on the fourth, and then blackcurrant juice on the fifth, after which I wanted nothing but water for two days and then the wretched routine started all over again. It was not the lack of alcohol which worried me because that has never been of any great concern to me. It was the process of absorbing these juices and mixtures which, among other things, had such a depressing effect. However, after six months champagne was permitted and life began to take on a rather brighter hue. But for a year or more I still felt the effects of this attack and in order to avoid any recurrence I was told to limit the load of work I was carrying. Since 1955 I had been Government Chief Whip, and in 1959 I became Minister of Labour with a seat in Harold Macmillan's Cabinet. In July 1960 I was appointed Lord Privy Seal at the Foreign Office.

However good the advice about limiting the work load, this was more easily said than done, for almost immediately I became involved in handling the first negotiations for Britain's entry into the European Community. Next I took charge of one of the great departments of State, becoming Secretary of State for Industry, Trade, and Regional Development. By 1965, the year in which I became Leader of the Opposition, I was almost fifty, and again I was being told that I could not go on indefinitely at the pace I had been living for the previous twenty years if I wanted to carry heavy political burdens in future. 'You had better be sensible now' I was told – so, in that early summer in Broadstairs, I was looking around for a way of being so.

It was good to be back in Broadstairs for a day that weekend and, as always, I walked along the cliffs from my home down on to the jetty. It was a pleasant sunny afternoon and the Channel was in one of its quieter moods. The tide was in and some boats were

15

floating on their moorings with the water softly lapping round them. Others were already being rigged by their crews, the mainsails were flopping on their booms, dinghies on trailers were being wheeled off the jetty across the sand to the water's edge, and already some hopefuls were trying to make the best use they could of a light breeze in the bay. I took a look over this bustling scene as I had done so many times before and went on with my stroll. I turned to find what seemed to me a new development, a small kiosk standing there with 'Viking Sailing School' written over it. In front of it stood a stocky, sunburnt, dark-haired man whom I had not met before. Seeing me look at his enrolment centre he pointed to it and said: 'If you are interested in sailing, why not start here?'

As a boy I had always wanted to sail, but in those days the opportunities were nothing like as numerous as they are today. There was a sailing club in Broadstairs before the Second World War and small boats began to appear in the harbour. The majority of craft were cabin cruisers and motor boats used for fishing. There were also two or three larger boats owned by local boatmen who used them to earn their living by taking visitors round the bays or out to the Goodwins in summer, and for fishing or getting their lobster pots in the rest of the time. The most famous of these was the *Perseverance,* and whenever I find myself racing against Sir Max Aitken's boat of that name I still think of her. Alas, she was stolen one night some years ago. She was picked up by a passing freighter and she went down through being towed too fast. The boatmen today are a dwindling number, but they are my friends. Some I knew at school, like Jack Croom, whose son is now in Lloyds but still takes out a boat when we go fishing off the Foreland.

There were very few boys at that time sailing dinghies; those there were I envied. Nor did there seem to be any idea of young people clubbing together to buy a boat cheaply to race in the dinghy classes. In any case even that would have been beyond my means. I tried to satisfy my own longings, as so many young people have done throughout time, by voraciously reading the sailing periodicals, occasionally, when there were special numbers, buying them for myself, but usually devouring them in the reading room of the small local public library. When I returned home after the war I helped to refound the sailing club, but that was as far as I had got.

My real delight had been to watch the big J–class boats from the shore when they came to the Royal Temple Yacht Club Regatta at Ramsgate in the thirties. At that time the Regatta lasted a week and was included by most of the big boats in their programme round the coast before and after Cowes Week. They were a splendid sight with full sail up in a good breeze competing for the Ramsgate Gold Cup — the Town Cup. I was not to know then that thirty years later we would win that cup, under very changed conditions, in the first *Morning Cloud*. I was fortunate, too, in spending holidays around the Solent, either on the mainland or in the Isle of Wight. Always, everywhere, there were boats to be seen. I spent hours and hours wandering round the outer harbour wall at Ramsgate and the inner basin, or looking at the moorings at Seaview and Bembridge, fascinated by the activity going on there.

Now, on the jetty at Broadstairs, I had a chance of getting down to sailing seriously. Should I take it? I had music as a recreation, concert going, opera, piano playing, conducting a concert once a year and listening to stereo, but that was a spiritual experience. I had nothing physical except swimming. I had given up golf some years before because I found that inevitably people talked politics; I could never get away from it. Not that I was ever competent at the game; indeed living in an area surrounded by championship courses I feel some embarrassment at my inability to cope with it successfully. Would I be any better at sailing? After all, I was then a year off becoming fifty. Gordon Knight, the owner of the little kiosk, was very persuasive, and I settled with him on the spot. We began to talk boats and how to sail them. And that is how it all began.

Ramsgate in a high gale, from an early nineteenth-century print

How much did I know about it already? he asked rather cautiously. I replied that I had done some small boat sailing but that was in Brittany when I was staying with the Seligmans, friends of my Oxford days, who had a cottage on the harbour wall at St Jacut-de-la-Mer. We had messed around in a small French dinghy called a 'Vaurien'. On one occasion we had even raced to St Briac in a somewhat choppy Brittany sea, but I could not claim that we had been well placed. Yes, I had both crewed and steered in the early fifties, but all in all would it not be better now if I started from scratch, if he assumed that I knew nothing and had to be taught everything? Gordon Knight readily agreed. I arranged to get down to the boat on either a Saturday or Sunday each weekend and planned to spend almost the whole of August sailing there.

I began on a boat of a local class, a Foreland one design. I doubt whether there is anything better for most beginners, especially if they are not all that young, than to get hold of one of their local class boats for a start. I now realize more than ever what an enormous advantage it is to start in one's teens, or even earlier. Young children can easily learn on a single-sail small boat like the Optimist, which is now a world-wide class; or if they are a bit older they can start in a Cadet or Mirror, tens of thousands of which are afloat today. They are reasonably priced and children can club together to buy them second-hand. At that age, after some preliminary instruction at a sailing school, their reactions are almost automatic and their reflexes very quick. They get used to a boat capsizing and quickly righting it again. As a result they become quite uninhibited in handling a small boat, they become both self–confident and independent, they develop an eye for the sudden opportunity in racing and they get used to taking it aggressively. There is everything to be said for starting young in sailing.

The Foreland class at Broadstairs is a heavy boat, sixteen feet overall with a partly covered-in foredeck. As such it is too weighty to trail up and down the beach and lies on its moorings throughout the summer. It crews three and is immensely stable. Originally designed in America by E. G. Monk in 1932 as the Curlew, the first nine boats built in Essex were delivered to Broadstairs in 1948. The class has proved its worth. It is a boat in which one can really have confidence. There remain some fourteen still in the class nearly thirty years after it began. In this, of course, the Foreland is not unusual. Many a local class has lasted as long as this and some longer. It is one of the advantages of class racing that, once instituted, it can go on as long as the boats last. They may not be fashionable or necessarily as fast as later designs, but they have their own characteristics and their owners swear by them.

True to his word, the following weekend Gordon Knight started me from scratch. We began by preparing the boat, getting the headsail hanked on ready to hoist, and the mainsail along the

On board *Flamingo*, a North Foreland one design class, at her moorings in Broadstairs harbour. Gordon Knight, the sailing instructor, is in the stern

boom. With the rudder and tiller dropped into position we were ready to move off. This was always a somewhat tricky manoeuvre, first to get *Flamingo,* as she was called, through the rows of other boats moored in the harbour. This required a good deal of fending-off and the help of an oar to paddle us out. It also meant that when we hoisted the sails we had to be sure we had already got some searoom. This was particularly necessary when we had a south-easterly, for if we did not have a chance to get sufficient leeway on moving away from the shore we were liable to be blown broadside on to the beach. From the moorings, however, we were normally able to achieve this successfully, get both the headsail and the mainsail up together with the help of the third member of the crew who usually came from the sailing club, and then go out into the bay where we could then start tacking.

Weekend after weekend I gradually became more involved in the more obvious practicalities of sailing a small boat. Using the sheet to play the headsail if I was in charge of that, or playing the mainsheet if I was amidships on the boat; setting them speedily when we tacked and using weight to keep the boat balanced. There was a good deal of ribald commentary at the time about my weight in a small boat and I reckoned that I had better do something about getting it down. As the weekends went by we found ourselves gybing – somehow a manoeuvre which always has an element of uncertainty in it for every sailor. In bad conditions there is some element of risk in it for small boats and of danger for the crews of bigger ones.

Then came the moment when I was invited to take the helm. I did not press for this but it was the moment I had been waiting for. In the summer holidays in Brittany I had taken it occasionally and immensely enjoyed controlling a small boat. Now I found that I liked having the feel of a boat under my hand and a crew who could trim the sails to our course. More than that, I was able to concentrate on handling the boat in a way which appealed to me more than just playing the sheets on the sails.

All this was fairly rudimentary stuff. What made the weekends so interesting was that intermixed with the instruction were races for the Foreland class. At that time the club raced every Saturday and Sunday as well as on two evenings in the week. Usually there were six or seven classes out of which the Forelands were by far the heaviest. That gave us an advantage in a good blow as we remained steadier and at least a bit drier than the more adven- turous sports in Hornets and Merlins, or other crews out on a trapeze. It was in this racing that I began to get some experience of tides and eddies around the shore and realized to the full how important local knowledge is when sailing in British waters. It is also one of the reasons why sailing is such a difficult sport for spectators to understand, unless they watch it on a television screen with a commentator who really knows what he is about.

To see a boat round a buoy and head straight for the next buoy on the course is understandable and seems logical and sensible. To see a competitor round a buoy and then head inshore, take a much longer route to arrive at the second buoy but do so earlier than its rival is puzzling unless you know that inshore the tide has already turned and is in fact carrying the second boat along. At Broadstairs we have a series of seven bays where we can use the tide or dodge the tide as circumstances demand. Every bay has its rocks and rock-hopping is an essential part of the sport. It requires a knowledge of every bunch of rocks sticking up along the coast, as well as an immediate readiness to pull up the centreboard if by misjudgement you unluckily hit one of them. If all that is not enough there is the long slipway running out from the jetty which it often paid us to try to slide across at high tide in order to get over the finishing line at the point nearest to the Committee box with the race officer ready to give us a gun.

The two most difficult problems were those which face every sailor racing, manoeuvring on the start line for a favourable position with the wind and the tide where one could not be baulked by a rival; and secondly, judging when to tack off in order to fetch a mark. The temptation with the first was not to allow enough time for the Foreland to pick up sufficient speed to reach the line within a few seconds of the starting gun; the temptation with the second was not to make enough allowance for the impact on the boat of the very powerful tides swirling around the rocks. Either we tacked too soon with the tide against us and found ourselves going on tacking all the way out to the buoy, often encountering great difficulty in getting round it at all; or, with the tide behind us, we went on too far, were carried further down than we needed and wasted time by overstanding the mark. I still think it is the most difficult judgement to make in sailing.

That was a happy summer. We had some success racing, though not when we took part in the Royal Temple Yacht Club's Regatta. From it I learnt the basic skills of handling a small boat which have always stood me in good stead. As I became more and more interested I seized every book I could find about small boat sailing and read them, even though much of what was written did not at that time concern me. One thing became more and more clear. An intellectual understanding of what sailing is about, what drives a boat, what tactics can achieve, all provide a mental stimulus, a foundation for action and an endless source of argument. But in this books are no substitute for experience. I have always found it a good thing to question every proposition which the local sailors put to me – such as, that unless you go aground once in three when you are racing, you are not really trying. Question it intellectually because all that the dogma indicates is gross incompetence in going aground. Question it from experience because having done it once it is unforgiveable not to learn from that experience and avoid doing it again.

Sailing at Broadstairs.
Above: Getting the Snipe
Blue Heather back in
position on Broadstairs
jetty after racing and
washing down, 1967. Right:
Rigging Madron Seligman's
Enterprise, 1968. Following
pages: Rigging the Snipe at
Broadstairs, 1967. Fireballs
are drawn up on the beach
in the background. *Blue
Heather II* was to be a
Fireball, an exciting boat to
sail

3 Small Boats

There was obviously no point in thinking of buying my own dinghy during that first season 'under instruction'. Instead I bought a small speedboat, a Glastron, with a 100 h.p. Evinrude engine, which I named *White Heather*. She could do some 25 knots in a reasonably smooth sea – provided her bottom was clean.

She was too heavy to trail to the beach and had to lie on moorings in the harbour where I rapidly learnt how quickly even a hull covered with anti-fouling paint can attract that dark-green growth of marine vegetation. I found, too, how visibly a boat's speed increased after I had scraped the bottom and polished it hard. People sometimes wonder at the trouble crews take in getting their boats out of water, and cleaning and polishing their hulls, but when you are racing you cannot afford to lose even a fraction of a knot because of the extra friction which comes from a boat moving through the water with a dirty keel or hull. I used her for fishing, for towing water-skiers and for going off to picnics around the coast. When we were racing, others took her out as an additional safety boat for the club.

I then decided to buy my own boat to race during the next season and I started to look around for something suitable. *White Heather* was built of fibreglass and apart from keeping the bottom scraped required little maintenance. This was a great advantage over the wooden boats which comprised the majority of the fleet.

I was lucky. I heard that a fellow club member wanted to sell his Snipe, only two years old, built of fibreglass and in excellent condition. The Snipe is a world-wide class, sixteen feet overall, sailed by a helmsman with one crew, and well known as an all-weather boat. At that time the class at Broadstairs numbered fourteen – this was the newest and only fibreglass boat in the club. The Snipes always had good racing and had proved themselves well suited to the sort of seas we normally encountered.

I settled to buy the boat for £200 and went about persuading one or two members of the club to crew with me at weekends. She was coloured blue and I named her *Blue Heather*. We sailed her all through the season in 1967. I kept her on her trailer on the jetty. This meant a heavy slog getting her down on to the sands to launch her from the beach, but it did give us the opportunity of sailing no matter what the state of the tide. However, it also introduced the complication of getting the sails hoisted while she was lying on the edge of the water and then trying to push off into the bay without being blown back again. This problem brought about my first incident with *Blue Heather*.

To make sure that we would really be able to get away instead of being pushed by a south-easterly back into the sands, I headed from the beach towards the jetty between a row of moorings. She picked up speed at once. I tried to tack to get between a couple of boats but she was moving so fast that before I could do so her bow crashed into the side of the jetty – to the astonishment

of a crowd of onlookers peering down from above and to the fury of my crew who shouted fiercely: 'It's bloody well time I had a skipper who can go about before he hits a bloody great pier!'

At that moment I was glad about the fibreglass. The bow had stood up to it remarkably well with only a small chip off to one side. It did not prevent us racing that afternoon. After we had dropped sails and paddled our way out along the side of the jetty, we took good care to get well clear before making for the starting line. The bow was repaired in a couple of days by a local firm who charged me just over £5.

Early in the year I found her more difficult to handle than the Foreland. She reacted much more quickly to any change in the seas or the wind. One Saturday afternoon, as we were in a good position, sailing to the weather mark, a sudden gust came down the gap in the cliffs. The boat shot forward. My crew went right out over the gun in an attempt to balance us up. I went out as far as possible, but she still went on heeling. I was too slow in easing the mainsail sheet and over we went. The boat behind us, a Fireball, rounded the mark and did likewise.

Knowing how liable we were to capsize we had often gone through the drill, but on this occasion there was quite a bit of sea running and we found we could not get her upright again. At the first attempt she righted, but then she went over on the other side. At this point I made another mistake. One of the rules of the club was that at sea members should always wear a lifejacket of an approved type. Although often tempted not to do so in fine weather, I invariably wore mine, in part as a way of showing younger members that we should all of us stick to the rules. On this occasion, thinking it would make handling the boat from the water less tiring, I decided to pull the tag which inflated my jacket. What I had not realized until that moment was how difficult it then becomes to clamber up the side of an upturned dinghy. Moral – never fully inflate your lifejacket until you actually need it to keep you afloat.

By this time the tide was running more strongly, sweeping us north along the coast towards the jetty and somewhat out to sea. Not one of the safety boats was in sight and we had drifted something more than a mile and a half before the *Perseverance* appeared, took hold of the boat and dragged us out of the water. Meantime the mast had been bumping along the bottom and was badly buckled when the boat was finally brought upright. However, I was able to get a replacement early the following morning, we re-rigged the boat and got some more sailing that weekend. At the end of the season I sold her for £175. It seemed to me that I had had a very good summer's enjoyment for about £30 – probably far less than I would have paid in any other sport.

In the club a newer design was becoming popular, the Fireball. This class was increasing rapidly in numbers, particularly in North America, Australia and parts of Europe. Just over sixteen feet in

The Snipe racing at Broadstairs in 1967

length, it is a somewhat flat-bottomed boat which planes extremely well. It is an exciting boat to sail which requires much more skill in handling. One or two adventurous spirits had started by building their own from 'build-it-yourself' kits. A good many doubts were expressed as to whether these could stand up to the sort of punishment small boats got on our corner of the coast, but on the whole they had survived well. A few rudders had come adrift and one or two booms had been broken, but the general view now was that they had come to stay. A number of members were changing over to them and I decided to do likewise.

This time I wanted to get a new boat and went to Jack Chippendale in Fareham, near Portsmouth, the authorized builder of Fireballs, to discuss the project with him. I finally settled the question at the Boat Show in January 1968, and he produced a boat which was a delight to the eye and a joy to sail. With a fibreglass hull and polished wooden decking she had the right combination of materials for a practical and attractive boat. When she was completed I went down myself to collect her and trailed her along the south coast to Broadstairs where she became

Blue Heather II and the envy of many eyes.

The sailing that we got that summer was in many ways the most enjoyable I ever had in a small boat. Even in the lightest winds she could always be gently edged along. The set of sails presented to me when I visited Australia in August helped enormously in this. In a good breeze she skimmed along, but balancing the boat then became all-important. The crew, who was still loyally with me, could get out on the trapeze and with a steady wind all was fine.

About this time I was told that a warning had been received that an attempt would be made on my life. A security officer was attached to me at short notice as a precaution just before I drove to Broadstairs for the weekend. On Saturday when I went down to the jetty to rig *Blue Heather II* for racing it became apparent that he had not had time to equip himself in a way which would enable him to be taken as a natural member of the sailing fraternity. Indeed he stood out rather conspicuously among the holiday-makers on the beach. It was also obvious to me that he was worried as to how he was to carry out his obligation to protect me when I was in a Fireball. I solved the latter problem by asking one of the Sailing

Club members to take out *White Heather,* my speedboat, and suggesting that he should go in it while I raced. Having arranged that I concentrated on the job in hand.

It was only when we were coming up to the finishing line some two hours later that I realized what was happening. The customary group of photographers around the jetty had spotted this unusual figure in *White Heather,* and had put two and two together and drawn their own conclusions. Having hired one of the fishermen's boats, they were manoeuvring ahead of us – obviously to some purpose. Glancing over my shoulder I saw in a flash what it was. They were trying to line up a picture of *Blue Heather II* with me at the helm, and *White Heather* behind us, with its special cargo – that was to be the weekend picture for the press. They succeeded. On Monday morning the picture was splashed across the papers – with the story.

When I met my admirable protector again later that day I asked him whether he had seen any of his colleagues since he had been to sea. 'Yes,' he replied, rather sadly, 'and every single one of them shouted at me "Follow that damn dinghy – quick." ' Later, when I had become Prime Minister, those responsible for my protection became adept, with more warning and more experience, at merging into the scene, be it with boats, apparently as members of the crew, or in the concert hall, as musicianly companions of myself as conductor – quite apart from all their normal activities. They always told me they enjoyed their changing roles. They certainly carried them off well. No one could have been better served in this way than I was.

At the beginning of the winter I reviewed the situation. Fireball sailing had been pleasant but there had been too many occasions when racing had been cancelled or it had not been possible to get out in the boat because of weather conditions. For those who lived on the spot this did not greatly matter, but for me it was different. Having set aside the day for recreation and relaxation in a political life which was becoming ever busier, it was frustrating to find that day wasted, especially as it involved driving seventy-five miles each way to the coast and back. My crew was getting married and moving away from our home town. I thought I had better look around for something bigger so that no matter what the weather I could always sail as I had planned.

I was sorry about this in many ways. As we had no permanent moorings in our small harbour suitable for a larger boat it would mean basing ourselves elsewhere. I would miss the club and its companionship. Small, housed in a building originally a café but now leased from the local Council, dependent entirely on its own resources, it only survived because so many of its members were prepared to do a stint in serving behind the bar and running its social activities as well as organizing its racing. The subscription had to be kept low so that the young could afford to become members; those in authority on the local Council did not always

The Fireball *Blue Heather II* racing at Broadstairs, 1968. A practical and attractive boat, and one which planed well; she required skilful handling in gusty weather

seem as understanding or as sympathetic as they might have been; and so the club had to concentrate on raising funds by other means as well as providing lectures for training in seamanship.

In all this it was but one of many hundreds of clubs up and down the country meeting the needs of the enthusiasts and supported by them. It had the great merit that after racing it brought everyone together under the same roof for a pint of beer, an argument about what had gone wrong—or occasionally right!—and a continuing discussion about everything affecting small boats and those who sail them. For me this has always been one of the joys of sailing. Here a club serving one area has an immense advantage. It is the same at Burnham-on-Crouch on the east coat. In this respect sailing on the Solent almost always ends in an anti-climax. After crossing the finishing line boats all go their various ways, off to Lymington or Hamble or Gosport; only a few crews ever meet up in Cowes for the sort of talk which finishes off the day well and makes it all so much more worthwhile. It is a pity that on the Solent where there is everything else the heart could desire, this is missing.

4 The First Morning

A general view of the 1969 Boat Show with (above) a half-model of the first *Morning Cloud*, a new design by Sparkman and Stephens of New York, exhibited at the show

Cloud

In January 1969 I went to the Boat Show.

Blue Heather II had been sold for very nearly what she cost me. It almost broke my heart to part with her, she was so beautifully built and so lovely to look at. I trailed the Fireball back to Jack Chippendale and handed it over to him for the new owner.

When I went to the Boat Show I had no clear idea what I was looking for. Because of the unavoidable publicity I had to take a good look at pretty well everything on every stand so as not to arouse suspicion that I was after a particular boat and provoke the inevitable press comment that I was about to become an affluent yacht owner.

I certainly had no intention at that time of taking part in ocean racing, about which I knew very little. My interest had been aroused, however, by invitations to sail on some bigger boats during the previous season. The first to suggest that I should abandon dinghies for a day was Morgan Giles, a colleague in the House of Commons, who at that time had one of the first of the larger fibreglass boats to be built, called *Meridian*. He suggested that I might like to take part in the annual 'Round the Island' Race starting at Cowes early in the morning and racing westwards round the Isle of Wight back to the finishing line in Cowes.

I accepted with interest but with some apprehension as to what I might be expected to do. This was increased when I went on board and found that all the rest of the crew, like my host, were of Admiral's rank. We started with a very light breeze in which there was little to do except drift down the Solent. The difficulties of establishing a process of decision-making and a firm line of communication among a crew of such exalted rank then rapidly became apparent. Finally it was agreed that we would benefit from getting a breeze from the thermal by going into Gurnard Bay on the island shore. The helmsman gently eased *Meridian* into the bay only to find that there was no thermal there. We were forced to watch the rest of the fleet drift past us down to the Needles. When we were finally able to emerge from the bay we were just about last in the fleet except for *Marabu,* a large boat taken over from the German navy at the end of the Second World War and now manned by the Royal Navy from Her Majesty's Dockyard at Portsmouth.

Our complement of Admirals on board then decided to head for the opposite shore, the mainland. Here we were more successful and began to make progress, especially when we lifted our keel as we got into shallower water. *Marabu,* watching us closely, decided to follow our example. Alas, she was not aware that we had a lifting keel and suddenly we saw her go hard aground. My last vision of the stranded boat was of another Admiral sitting in a broad wicker chair in the stern vigorously exhorting the very large crew of sailors to jump up and down on the leeward side in an attempt to get her off, an attempt which seemed to be signally failing.

As so often happens in this race, once round the Needles we got a bit more breeze from a following wind. For the first time I saw a glorious picture of more than five hundred boats, all with brightly coloured spinnakers up, sailing on a calm sea against a bright blue, cloudless sky. I do not remember seeing anything to match it anywhere else in the world, not even in Sydney, Australia.

Hearing that I had done the 'Round the Island' Race, another parliamentary colleague, Richard Sharples, took me racing off Southsea, near Portsmouth, in his *Excalibur II,* another large fibreglass boat. It was the first time we got entangled with photographers in launches on the start line. Richard himself was on the helm and narrowly missed slicing a small boat full of cameramen in half. This seemed to be the only thing which made them desist from stopping under our bow or from getting in the way of tacking. In my experience, those photographers who specialize in taking pictures of boats racing know full well the positions they can take up without interfering with the boats, especially in light weather. Others, commissioned by papers because of their interest in a particular boat or its crew, show no realization of how much they can upset the concentration of those on board and, when there is very little breeze, actually impede the boat. Because the sea belongs to everyone it is taken for granted that it does not matter where anybody goes. On each *Morning Cloud* I have had a rule that no matter what happens we keep absolute silence. Nothing gives us more pleasure than when a neighbouring crew really tell these people where they get off, in language which is seldom ineffective. Onshore, over a drink, I sometimes ask the photographers what would happen if they went to an athletics meeting, donned spiked shoes and ran backwards around the track in front of the competitors in order to get a full head-on view when they were racing. Nonsensical, of course; but it is what happens to us out racing on innumerable occasions. Perhaps our friends the photographers could remember this – and even recognize that in a light breeze the wash from their launch can kill a boat stone dead.

Richard Sharples and his family proved to be good sailing friends. On my recommendation the Queen appointed him Governor of Bermuda in 1972, where he was a great success. It was a terrible blow to me personally, as well as a national loss, when he was assassinated only a few months after he went to that island, itself so well known for its sailing and the teams it has produced for the Admiral's Cup.

My first ocean race was in *Clarion of Wight,* a boat owned by Maurice Laing which had earlier won the Fastnet Race. Hearing that I had been sailing on bigger boats he kindly sent me an invitation to do an ocean race with him, indicating that he thought I would find the race from Cowes to Dinard probably the most enjoyable as a first go. I accepted his invitation. The night before the race we stayed in Southampton, and early on Friday morning went across to Cowes where his crew was already on board.

Once again there was precious little wind. This time we started to the east, having then to go through the forts off Portsmouth, which I have since got to know so well, and then round the Nab Tower before making for the French coast. After a time I was given the helm and with the aid of a very lightweight headsail we got the boat moving. Much to everyone's surprise I overtook another boat under her lee before rounding the Nab and began to feel quite pleased with myself.

Clarion was well furnished below and I was given a comfortable bunk aft. That evening we were served some delicious steaks for dinner, together with some excellent claret. I began to enjoy myself still more. When I came up to do the watch from four to eight o'clock in the morning there was still only a light breeze, but we were moving quite well. In the middle of the watch someone said: 'Let's throw over a line or two to catch mackerel for breakfast.' Freshly cooked these make one's mouth water.

During Saturday the wind got up and we finally sailed over the finishing line in Dinard late that evening and then went into the dock at St Malo. There was no question of staying on board in the dock; off we went to a comfortable French hotel where I and the crew of *Morning Cloud* have stayed after every race since. The next morning the port of St Malo was a magnificent sight. The dock was crowded with boats, most of them flying spinnakers to dry them out. The dockside was crowded with families and holidaymakers taking their Sunday morning stroll – a picture of light and colour against the grey walls of the old fortress town.

'If this is what ocean racing means,' I said to myself, 'then I am for it' – but I have never experienced anything quite like it since. The Cowes–Dinard Race remains one of the most enjoyable of our ocean races, very largely because it finishes not only at a different port, but in a different country. Even though they may go along the French coast at some point or other, almost all our other races finish very close to where they started.

Later, in *Morning Cloud*, we were to have our Cowes–Dinard traditions – to get in to St Malo in time for a late supper at the Duchesse Anne; cross the bay to Dinard on Sunday morning for lunch at the Hotel Printania, which tends to last well into the afternoon; and then over to the Yacht Club for the customary champagne and the presentation of the prizes.

On three occasions we were to win our class in *Morning Cloud*, but never yet have we succeeded in winning the Cowes–Dinard Race overall. In 1973 we thought we had finally done it in the third *Morning Cloud*. *Quailo*, another member of the 1973 British Admiral's Cup team, was our closest rival and when we crossed the finishing line she was already in. Imagine our delight when Anthony Churchill, my navigator, calculated that by corrected time we were two-and-a-half minutes ahead of them. After getting into the dock at St Malo and changing our clothes, we went off to the Duchesse Anne to find the crew of *Quailo* already there celebrating what they thought was their victory. Having indicated to them as delicately as we could the actual timings, we left a somewhat depressed dinner table and went ourselves to celebrate. That night I went happily to bed, only to be woken in the morning to be told that a small French boat had arrived home just before breakfast, easily beating both of us. It is incredible what the French can do in small ocean-racing boats.

But, to return to the 1969 Boat Show. Going round it I found two boats which I thought might suit me well. One, French, was thirty-one feet overall, an attractive hull, and well laid out below. It already had quite a racing record. The other was a new design by Sparkman and Stephens of New York. Nearly thirty-four feet overall, it was built of fibreglass and I was particularly impressed by the lines. As they looked so attractive I thought there was a good chance that the performance would live up to the lines. I did not go on board but I arranged to slip back alone later in the week to have a private look.

I had no one to advise me but when I next saw the S&S 34, as she was called, I felt instinctively that she was the right boat for me. When I went down below I found that she was well and comfortably fitted out, with the possibility of six bunks, including two cots in the forepeak, a reasonably sized galley and a satisfactory navigation table. The enclosed heads and washbasin were just forward of the mast and amidships was a dining table. Around it the bunks could be converted into seats which were well upholstered and covered with a hard-wearing vinyl material. She was finished below in teak, not only the woodwork but also the cabin sole. This gave her an air of stability and well-being.

Later, when we began racing seriously, this was to be the cause of continued controversy amongst the crew, especially the woodwork, the table and the upholstery of the bunks. How much did it weigh? they persisted in asking. How could anyone really concentrate on competitive sport when living in this sort of comfort? they demanded. To me, at the time, it all looked rather desirable. There was nothing skimped, or for that matter flashy. It just seemed common sense to finish the boat off in this way. Later my own views changed, as we shall see, and the first *Morning Cloud* is the only boat on board which we have ever had what so many people regard as the basic necessities of comfort.

As I sat on this comfortable upholstery below, thinking over the possibilities of buying it, a gentle, bespectacled figure came down the companionway. He was introduced to me by the salesman as the designer of the boat, Olin Stephens, a famous name, though at that time I knew little about him. We only exchanged a few sentences before he said he had to leave to catch a plane out of London. I asked him about the new S&S 34. Yes, he thought it was probably a good boat. Yes, he thought it would probably have a good performance. Yes, if I did have one he thought I would probably find it satisfactory. Then he disappeared. And

Olin Stephens (left), the designer of the first *Morning Cloud*, a production boat built on the Medway by Michael Winfield's firm

so began an acquaintanceship which developed into a working relationship and is now a close friendship between Olin Stephens, one of the world's greatest and most successful designers, and myself. He has been responsible for all four *Morning Clouds*.

That first encounter gave me the clue to his character. Quiet, modest, unassuming, almost diffident, he made no boastful claims for his new design; indeed he constantly qualified his assessment almost to the point of understatement. A soft sell? No, I did not feel it was so at the time and now I have known him for many years I am sure that it is the true character of the man himself.

How often people have asked me how *Morning Cloud* got her name! In fact, the name was already on the stern when I first saw her, but spelt as one word – *Morningcloud*. This was derived from *Morningtown,* a very successful one-tonner, also designed by Olin Stephens and owned by the builder of the new 34s, Mike Winfield. The name was taken from a popular song of the day and he had decided to continue the line. Sure enough it was followed and in succession there came *Morning After* – soon to be our fiercest rival – *Morning Glory, Morning Haze, Morning Melody, Morning Flame* and others. There was even a suggestion of *Morning All,* but by the exercise of a common act of telepathy we effectively drew the line at that!

For me, spelling the name as one word made no sense. I split it up.

That was how *Morning Cloud* came to be created. With all our ups and downs it has become probably the best-known name in sailing, a household word right across the world. Its most enchanting use I found in Hong Kong when I went there after winning the Sydney–Hobart Race. The Chinese newspapers greeted me with characteristic imagery in a banner headline, which translated read, 'The man who has come down from the Morning Cloud'. I have never numbered the boats. Each one has been just *Morning Cloud*.

5 A Good Season's Racing

Morning Cloud was launched at Upnor on the Medway, where she had been built, on 12 April 1969. At the first two attempts the bottle of champagne bounced off the bow. It was only at the third attempt that my stepmother succeeded in getting it to break. You can only be sure of success in this specialized field of launching ships by taking a firm grip of the bottle with one hand on the neck and the other on the base and then hurling it as violently as possible at your objective! Lowered into the water the boat was perfectly balanced and delightful to look at.

After the usual celebration party we set off down the Medway in a good breeze. I took the helm and felt very much at home. On this occasion the bevy of press men and photographers was far greater than we had ever had surrounding the dinghies. As she heeled well over in more than 20 knots of wind the photographs which appeared in the next day's press caused some alarm amongst well-wishers who were thinking of a General Election in 1970. To them this seemed to be a somewhat precarious weekend occupation. The boat was manned very largely by those connected with the firm who had built her. We took her out the next day,

Above: At the third attempt, the bottle hits the bow of the first *Morning Cloud* at her launching on the Medway, April 1969

Opposite: *Morning Cloud* racing in the Solent in 1969

Trouble with the halyards!
Anthony Law up the mast
during the second day of
trials with the first *Morning
Cloud* on the Medway

a Sunday, so that we could do some tuning. This, as I have come to appreciate more and more, is a fine art. The larger and more complex successive *Morning Clouds* have become, the more numerous are the different parts which may have to be adjusted.

There is the problem of getting the mast in precisely the right position, to make sure it is straight and not being pulled out of shape by the various tensions on it, and to give it just the right degree of rake for the sails to be able to set well. The backstay and the forestay must also be tuned. The forestay has to be taut so that it does not sag, allowing the headsail to become baggy, but instead is stiff, providing a firm support for the different positions of the headsail. Several thousands of pounds of pressure can be put on the backstay by various devices for tightening it, either by a simple screw turned by hand or by a hydraulic pump, also usually hand-operated. This will pull the mast back, so that the sails can be sheeted in tighter and hardened when sailing into the wind. All these devices can be released. The mast then springs forward again, when the boat is running before the wind, either with just a headsail or with the spinnaker up. The shrouds on each side of the mast holding it in position also need to be adjusted, and there are numerous other details which have to be attended to.

Then, there is the basic question of ballast in the boat. If the weight of lead in the keel is not sufficient to balance the boat properly, then more lead can be put into the bilges. In the last two *Morning Clouds* we left two square holes in the keel, one forward and one aft, which were fitted with blocks. We could then knock out one or both of them and replace them with lead if we wanted more weight in the keel. By this means we could add up to about eleven hundred pounds in extra weight. Finally there is the question of the effectiveness of the sails once they are set. Each sail-maker has his own patterns, and although most of them also have a means of flying the sails when they have been cut, it is never possible to say how effective they will be until they are actually being used on the boat. Only then can one see whether the cut is right and whether they suit each other.

All these different factors greatly affect the speed and performance of a boat. In an ideal world we would only adjust one thing at a time, try it out in different wind and sea conditions, carefully record all the circumstances and the results and then decide whether or not it was an improvement. But all too often there is no time for this and tuning a boat becomes to a large extent a matter of judgement and experience.

On this occasion I was told that the best hand at this in the whole country was coming up for the day to sail on *Morning Cloud* and do the necessary tuning. This was the first time I met Owen Parker. He certainly lived up to his reputation and he has played a prominent part in the life of successive *Morning Clouds* ever since. He went about tuning the boat with gusto. He went up the mast himself to check that all was well, came down and changed

First *Morning Cloud*. Above:
On trials in 1969 and (right)
in the Solent in the summer
of the same year

its rake, promptly proceeded to adjust the shrouds, and then turned his attention to the backstay. When we got under way he dealt with the sails and the general balance of the boat. For me it was a fascinating experience to watch him at work. If any man knows about tuning a boat and keeping it tuned, he does.

We were now getting ready for the racing season. Many of those connected with building the boat came from the east coast, so I thought we would start there and take the boat round to Cowes later on in the summer. On the east coast there are local races on the rivers, but there is also offshore racing in the North Sea and across to the coast of Northern Europe. Before I could be ready for this I had to get a permanent crew organized.

Here I was almost helpless. I knew no one well in the ocean-racing world, nor had I any idea how to get in touch with them. Here the boat-builder came to my aid. A flamboyant character whose interest was very largely in public relations, Mike Winfield promised me a first-rate crew for the first couple of races. To find out who they were and to get to know them I had a party in my flat off Piccadilly. We needed six for *Morning Cloud,* including myself, and with the promise of a party rather more turned up. They were certainly a distinguished lot and I thought we would be well prepared for whatever was to come. Among them was Anthony Churchill, who later became the navigator on the first three *Morning Clouds.*

I entered *Morning Cloud* for the first offshore race of the season on the east coast, the race for the Pattinson Cup. It started from West Mersea on the River Blackwater, went out into the North Sea and came back to Burnham up the River Crouch where I had moorings for the boat. It turned out to be a race I shall never forget.

Having taken the *Cloud* round to West Mersea and enjoyed a good Club dinner, we stayed ashore and went down to the boat early on the Saturday morning. The weather forecast was a light breeze dying away in the course of the day. While we were getting the boat ready for this early start, the launch came alongside and from it leapt a slight figure who introduced himself as Rod Stephens, Olin's brother. It was only the night before that I had heard that he might be able to sail with us, a pleasant surprise, for he had a world-wide reputation for handling boats and being able to make them go.

I watched him with interest. He was carrying only a small bundle, small enough to get his hand round. It turned out to be a pair of thin lightweight oilies wrapped round some tools. Having donned his oilies while we went on rigging the boat, he looked around and without any fuss started to get things ship-shape himself. It was obvious that nothing missed his eagle eye. A sheet in the cockpit was covered with mud from this mud-bank-ridden river. Having got the cockpit sorted out, he dipped the sheet over the side and washed that out. I could see that he believed in everything being spotless.

With Rod Stephens, a man
whose eagle eye missed
nothing

I learnt at once two lessons from him. That it is not necessary
for the crew to hump a lot of baggage on board every time they
sail; it is all extra weight which clutters up a small boat down
below and may very well make it more difficult to handle. But
what a job it is to stop it being brought on board! And it is even
more of a job to get lockers turned out regularly and the accumula-
tion of kit and personal belongings moved ashore. The other
lesson was the secret of Rod Stephens's continuing success, a
never-ending attention to detail.

We made a good start, the race got under way and it was soon
apparent that we were well placed. *Morning After,* the main rival
in our class, had gone close inshore and was obviously losing out
by doing so. Then the wind, instead of dying away, blew pro-
gressively stronger. By the time we were in the North Sea and had
rounded the furthest mark there was a big sea running, and as
we began the leg home to Burnham we had some 30-35 knots of
wind across the deck. The channel up the River Crouch is comparatively narrow, especially on a falling tide. On each side of it
are mud banks which were now being churned up by the short,
heavy seas. The art was to get as near as one could to the mud
bank before tacking, with the ever-present risk of going aground
and being stuck there until the next flood tide. This was not a
pleasant prospect in that sort of weather.

After we had headed for home we were slowly overtaken by the
biggest boat in the race, *Cervantes 3.* It was surprising how long
she had taken to catch up with us. We were both on starboard
tack, but shortly after she passed us she tacked to port and we
lost sight of her in the mist and rain. Able to go a bit closer in
towards the mud than *Cervantes,* we went on further before we
tacked. To our astonishment, we saw ahead of us this splendid
boat dis-masted, spars and sails over the side, wallowing like a
great bird with broken wings in the stormy sea. In all the noise
we had heard nothing as her shrouds parted and the mast went.
It was obvious that the crew were safe and there was nothing we
could do. As we went past they waved us on.

In these conditions it became a longer race. Instead of getting
back in time for the Club dinner, it was well after dark before we
finally tied up on our moorings. As we went ashore Rod Stephens
said to me: 'I expect they will have kept something for us to eat,
but it will be a long time before the rest of them get in. They may
want us to wait so that they can give us all a meal together. Do
you want me to go over the points I have got about the boat
before we eat or afterwards?'

'Points about the boat?' I said. 'What do you mean?'

'I've made a note of everything which ought to be done to her,'
he replied. 'I think I've got a couple of dozen altogether. I would
like to go through them with you.' I was astonished.

Tired, soaked to the skin and hungry, I said I would rather have
a bath, change into something dry and then eat first.

'And you,' I said to Rod, 'must want some food as well, because I noticed you ate nothing all day on board except an apple. Why didn't you have any sandwiches? Surely the weather wasn't so bad that you couldn't eat them?'

'I'll tell you exactly why,' said Rod. 'When I was a young man I crewed on Mr Vanderbilt's boat. One day, when we were racing, the usual sumptuous lunch was served. Going below to eat it distracted our attention from the business in hand. When I came up I found that unbeknown to all of us our bitterest rival had slipped through us. We never caught her. Mr Vanderbilt was furious. Never again, he said, would we go below for lunch in a race; we would always stay on deck. And from that moment,' added Rod Stephens, 'when I've wanted something on a day race I've either eaten an apple or drunk some squash.'

And from that moment on we have done the same on *Morning Cloud*. There is a strange bit of psychology about all this. If you are eating a sandwich and you have to leap suddenly into action on a boat, the automatic reaction is still to try to protect the sandwich. The job does not get done speedily or as well as it could be. If you only have a half-eaten apple in your hand no one seems to mind dropping it and getting on with the job. Apples and Mars Bars are our staple diet when we are racing.

Although it was late when we finished our meal, Rod Stephens insisted on going through all the points he had noted about the boat that night before going to bed. I have seen since that this is a technique he follows whenever he is on board, no matter what the conditions. As I remember it, he had some twenty points on his list, some of them highly technical. When I started to write this account of the first *Morning Cloud* I asked him whether he still had his notes. By return of post there came from New York, six years after the event, a typed transcript of the points he had noted down and discussed after that race – in fact, twenty-four in all. I congratulated him on his filing system!

During our discussion the results came in. *Morning Cloud* had won her first offshore race in her class. We had almost won overall but we were just beaten by *Mersea Oyster,* a bigger boat in the class above us. It had been an exhilarating day and I had learnt a lot about the boat, about racing in rough weather, and about myself. Above all I had seen how one of the most experienced sailors in the world went about this job of offshore racing.

We did the return race a fortnight later and we were just beaten by *Morning After*. It happened at the last mark. We were leading until then but having tacked round the buoy we found that the headsail we had hoisted had been sheeted inside the shrouds instead of outside them. Changing over the sheet cost us precious time. We lost the race by just over a minute. It proved to those of us who did not know it already that even on a thirty-five-mile race every second counts. One bit of bad drill can ruin the rest of the day's performance and throw away a good result.

Red Rooster, winner of the 1969 Admiral's Cup. Dick Carter designed it and took the helm himself

The time had come to move *Morning Cloud* round from the east coast to the Solent where I had moorings on the River Hamble. This meant almost a complete change of crew. 1969 was Admiral's Cup year. Some of the crew, like Dave Johnson, who had been steering, and Anthony Churchill, the navigator, were going off to bigger boats taking part in the trials; others were returning to their own boats on the east coast. I had not realized before that the crew would dissolve in quite this way, but most of them had friends and contacts down in the south who were prepared to take part in at least some of the races during the summer.

Geoffrey Williams, who had just won the Solo Transatlantic Race in *Sir Thomas Lipton*, became my navigator. A Cornishman, he had already demonstrated his qualities in this sphere and was always tingling with fresh ideas about how to handle a boat. Yet I could feel that he was fundamentally a loner and this seemed to me to show itself unconsciously in an interesting way. As I watched him he always appeared to be making a careful calculation as to how long it would take to carry out a manoeuvre or make some adjustment if he were alone on the boat and had to do it on his own. He was a most stimulating person to have on board and everybody felt that he had been through so much in his Transatlantic race that no situation could possibly arise which he had not encountered previously.

Now that I had got my own boat, for sentimental reasons I particularly wanted to do the Cowes–Dinard Race. Once again we only had a light breeze but we did well round the Nab Tower. Then, having tacked in towards the Isle of Wight we tacked out again across the Channel. I have a vivid memory of looking astern and seeing that we were being rapidly overtaken by a larger boat at an unbelievable speed. It was the American boat *Red Rooster,* designed by Dick Carter. It passed us with all the crew sitting up to weather. Dick himself was at the helm. I was immensely impressed. In August *Red Rooster* won the Fastnet Race. Later on I got to know Dick Carter well. In many ways we had the same outlook towards the organization of a boat, its crew, and its racing. He often told me that he felt I was trying to do politically for Britain what he was engaged in doing with boat design and ocean racing on both sides of the Atlantic. Each of us was trying to change attitudes, perhaps faster than was generally acceptable. He had great success with his boats.

That Cowes–Dinard Race ended in thick fog. For the last two or three hours we were all on deck wearing life jackets. The safety gear was ready in case we were run down by some ship heading for St Malo. Geoffrey Williams' navigation was brilliant. Peering into the murky darkness we saw a faint line of lights gradually emerging. By the time they had any power we were on top of them. They were the lights of the frigate on station as the Committee boat. Geoffrey Williams had taken us straight to the finishing line. After we crossed it we made an attempt to find the channel in to the dock in St Malo, but it was hopeless. We dropped anchor for the night in the fog alongside a group of unknown boats. We had some satisfaction in hearing later that while we did so Anthony Churchill, navigating *Phantom,* one of the British Admiral's Cup team, was circling around, only a few hundred yards away, still looking for the finishing line.

That summer gave me my first experience of Cowes Week. As a sailing and social occasion it has been described on innumerable occasions with enthusiasm by sailors and with cynicism by commentators. On *Morning Cloud* we were far too busy to be able to pay much attention to anything except getting ourselves organised for the racing. We took part in the Channel Race over the first weekend. Like many another Channel race it gave us a good blow along the French coast. For me it was notable for two things. We were joined by Jean Berger, a Swiss living in London. He was an outstanding helmsman and had been British national Hornet champion. He was later to play a major part in our fortunes. Secondly, we were mortified to find that we had a leak in

Outside the Royal Yacht Squadron clubhouse at Cowes. Races are started from here, and it is the best place to watch an exciting finish

our fuel tank about which we were able to do nothing. As a result derv ran down into the bilges until it slopped all over the floor of our small cabin. The smell of derv was everywhere. For two thirds of the Channel Race we were plagued by this all-pervasive stomach-raising stench. But as one of the crew said afterwards, 'If you can spend forty-two hours on board a small boat in those conditions without being seasick, then you can sail anywhere.'

At the end of Cowes Week we set out on the Fastnet Race – my first. This took us from Cowes across to the Fastnet Rock in Southern Ireland and then back round the Scillies to Plymouth. Part of every day during Cowes Week was taken up with working out how much food we should need, getting in the stocks and trying to make sure we had not overlooked anything required for a race of well over six hundred miles which might take anything up to five days, depending on the weather. The crew was somewhat improvised. I had a navigator whom I had not met before and on the Thursday evening one of the crew on whom I was relying as a helmsman cried off. Fortunately I was able to persuade Jean Berger to change his business arrangements, rush down from London and join us at the last moment.

It turned out to be a fairly light Fastnet Race until we got near the Rock itself. Long before then misfortune struck. Not for the first time I was to find myself entangled in Irish affairs.

Long-distance radio had been installed on the boat so that, as Leader of the Opposition, I could keep in touch with my colleagues at home. Parliament had risen for the Summer Recess, but it was quite possible for a situation to develop about which they would want to consult me.

On the first day out Reggie Maudling, the Deputy Leader of the Party, whom I had left in charge, talked to me over the radio telephone to tell me about the outbreak of disturbances in Northern Ireland and the action the Labour Government was taking. We knew that the use of this powerful radio was quite a drain on our batteries, and directly the conversation had finished the engine was started to re-charge them.

On the second day out Reggie Maudling telephoned again to read over to me a somewhat lengthy statement he was proposing to issue. When I had agreed it and our conversation had finished I told the crew to go through the same procedure again. This time the engine refused to start. 'Now I suppose we haven't got a starting handle,' said one of the crew. With considerable satisfaction I replied, 'Yes we have. I checked it myself before we left and here it is.' It was true. I had checked it and there it was. What I had not done – and neither had anybody else – was actually to start the engine with the handle. When the crew went to do so they found that the engine was so placed amidships that it was impossible to get the starting handle into its socket without first removing the mast!

This was a shattering blow. The boat-builders had obviously

never examined it. We looked at it from every angle and considered every possibility but there was no getting away from it, there was no means by which we could do anything.

Precious little was left in the battery to feed our navigation instruments and soon there was no power left even for our navigation lights. We could make do by sailing without instruments; in fact many would say it was a good thing to be forced into that position. Not having navigation lights, however, meant that we could never claim our rights at sea; indeed we thought it only sensible to keep clear of every other boat which came near us. After we rounded the Scillies – it would be more accurate to say threaded our way through the rocks of the Scillies, for this was allowed under the rules at that time – we found ourselves at a great disadvantage.

I learnt the lesson very quickly. Since then a double battery system has been installed on every *Morning Cloud* and I have always refused to have an engine unless it could be started by hand and placed in the boat where there was plenty of room to swing the handle. As for the first *Morning Cloud*, the engine was adapted so that we could start her from the rear and a double battery system was installed as well.

Sailing for the rest of the season consisted of a weekend at Ramsgate – three miles from my home – where, although soundly beaten in the 'Round the Goodwins' Race on the Saturday – a race we were to win in 1974 with the third *Morning Cloud* – we won the Ramsgate Gold Cup on the Sunday. We went on to Burnham-on-Crouch, where our adventures had begun, for Burnham Week. Racing was excellent but we were far from satisfied with the performance of the boat. The first three days we spent every evening arguing about the changes we could make to improve its performance. Morale got lower and lower. I was in despair.

Then Owen Parker, who had first tuned the boat, reappeared on the scene to sail with us for the second half of the week. He listened to all our woes and heard the various proposals we were considering. The next morning he took a firm grip on the situation. As we went down to the starting line he said very forcibly in the hearing of the whole crew, 'Look, sir, you've got this bloody boat. Stop arguing about it and sail the bloody boat you've got. Then we might begin to get somewhere.' This put an end to all the arguments. Morale rose again. We came second in that race and on the last day, although he had then left us, we won. It was due to the impact of a remarkable personality. There always comes a point when you have to stop arguing about the boat and concentrate on sailing what you have got.

When we did have a success we had a simple tradition. We went ashore together for a meal in the evening. Down on the Hamble we used to go to the Bugle more often than not. We could sit and eat looking out over the peace and quiet of the Hamble River. Early in the summer, after rather a good day's racing, we were relaxing over our coffee when one of the crew said, 'Why don't we go off to Australia and do the Sydney–Hobart Race? We might do rather well.' Heady with our day's success, we said, 'Why not?' I must confess I joined in the chorus without having any realization of what would be involved. That night the germ of an idea was planted. That night started us on the path to a notable victory.

Back home we started having regular crew meetings to discuss every aspect of the venture – the familiar phrase 'think tank' came into use. There were a large number of points to be considered. First, we wanted to find out what we could about the previous twenty-four races from Sydney to Hobart. No one had more information about this than Olin and Rod Stephens. They put their staff on to making an analysis of the conditions under which the race had taken place in previous years. Later they, too, compared notes with Chris Bouzaid.

Then we had to study the Australian requirements for the races. There were some notable differences between their practice and

49

ours. In particular, their safety requirements were much more strict than those in Britain. Everybody had to have long-distance radio on board – though that did not worry us because we already had it – and had to report their position three times a day to the control boat moving down with the fleet from Sydney to Hobart. Some of the medical supplies stipulated were actually forbidden to us in British waters – they would have to be bought out there.

The crew had to be flown out to Australia. Quantas were willing to give us a substantial reduction in the cost of the fares for the whole party; British Overseas Airways could not help in any way. Once there, the crew would have to be accommodated both in Sydney and in Hobart, and accommodated together. We always felt that gave us the best crew spirit; we never liked being broken up. Here, Syd Fisher, captain of the subsequent Australian Admiral's Cup team, was helpful, arranging for us all to stay in a new hotel his company had just built. Then there were such prosaic details as getting hold of a really effective anti-sunburn lotion to protect us from the intense Australian sun. Incidentally, we settled for a thick paste called pinki-zinc which, liberally applied, gave us the general appearance of rather pale Red Indians with hair and eyebrows piercing through it.

The main question we faced was how to ensure that *Morning Cloud* had the best chance of doing well in the race. We discussed this at innumerable think tanks week after week, usually after a day's racing. Burnham Week gave us the chance of talking about it continuously night after night. After we went back to our homes and our jobs in September, we continued to meet in my flat in Albany. The crew tended to divide into two camps and finally I had to settle the argument myself, just in time to allow the necessary alterations to be made to the boat.

The argument was in fact a basic one which faces every owner and every designer when they are considering together what sort of boat to build. One school of thought said that we should first discover in what conditions the majority of races had been held over the past twenty-five years. We should then adapt the boat so that it could win in these conditions. If things in our particular race turned out differently, we would then probably find ourselves at the end of the fleet, but that was just too bad. The proponents of this doctrine were promptly labelled extremists by their opponents, largely because they wanted the boat to be pushed to her furthest limits by means of the adaptations they favoured. On average, the Sydney–Hobart Race has been a downwind race. They wanted us to increase the size of our spinnakers and head-sails to the maximum which could possibly be carried, accepting in the process the consequent penalties which would increase the rating – or handicapping – of the boat.

The other school of thought believed in trying to produce a boat which would do well in any set of conditions, though she might be beaten by one which was better suited to those in which the race happened to be held that year. In other words, they wanted an all-round boat as suitably equipped as possible.

We found, after carefully scrutinizing the rules as they existed at that time, that, in either case, we could do two things to the boat which would reduce our rating. The first was to put bands of steel round the inside of the boat. For historical reasons this reduced the rating significantly. From our own point of view it considerably strengthened our fibreglass boat and would be of great benefit to us in the heavy seas off the Bass Straits and the Tasmanian coast. The other 'trick' we could use to bring down the rating was to cover the deck with teak. This would be expensive and of no particular help to us from the sailing point of view. I decided that we would put in the 'stringers' – as the steel bands are called – but that we would not have the teak decking.

In the end, having listened to all the arguments, I decided that I would increase the sail area of the boat but not to the extent proposed by the extremists. Olin Stephens originally thought that *Morning Cloud* was perfectly satisfactory as she was, but later accepted our point of view and advised us as to how to do it. It meant increasing the length of our spinnaker poles and carrying bigger spinnakers as well as larger headsails. In the event we were very glad we did it, but at the think tank Jean Berger, who had pressed me to go as far as possible, had the last word when he said, 'I thought we'd been working on the assumption that we were sending *Morning Cloud* halfway across the world in order to win the Sydney–Hobart Race. I'm not at all sure now that we shall be able to do it.'

At Port Hamble they put in a hard week's work. Inserting the steel stringers meant dismantling and then reassembling the furnishing below deck. We did consider stripping down and removing all the teak panelling in order to save weight and lighten the boat. We could then have installed just four cots for the crew to sleep in. *Morning After* had been bought as a finished hull but never completely furnished below deck, and we sometimes wondered whether this gave her a better light-wind performance than *Morning Cloud*. It certainly gave us the opportunity to pull their legs. Of course it is entirely a matter for them, we said, if they liked to sleep in straw boxes; but before they asked us on board we did wish they would sometimes change the straw! Once again it was the 'extremists' who wanted to remove everything below. We compromised by taking out the movable equipment, such as the heavy teak table, but otherwise leaving her as she was. Port Hamble also checked over the whole boat and tested the equipment for strength. The rod rigging, a comparatively recent innovation at that time, was found to have contracted in diameter by a fraction of an inch. It was too late to get a new set made in time to travel with the boat. It went separately by air. *Morning Cloud* was then dismantled and taken by trailer to Tilbury to be shipped to Australia.

6 The Sydney

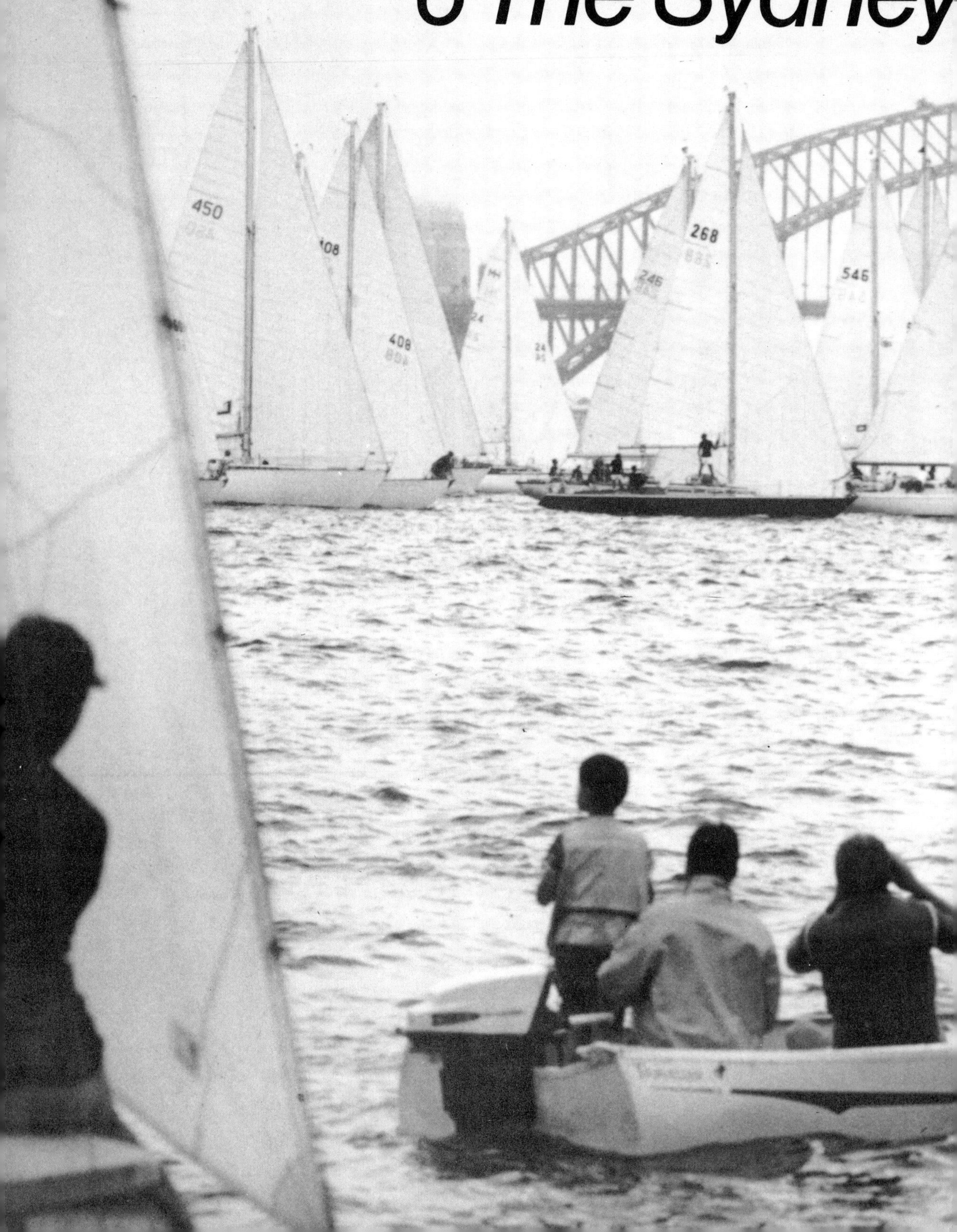

Hobart Race

Previous pages: The
spectacular Sydney harbour
bridge frames a group of
competitors at the start of
the 1969 Sydney-Hobart
Race. *Morning Cloud* is
second from the right

The more I thought about it the more I wanted to take part in the Sydney–Hobart Race. I had spent three weeks in Australia in August the previous year. I had been able to see a large part of the country, from the new mining developments in the north-west, to Melbourne, Sydney, and Brisbane in the east. It was not only enjoyable, it was immensely stimulating. My admiration both for Australia and for Australians was unbounded. On the other hand, many of the Australians to whom I had spoken had not bothered to conceal their view that Britain was pretty well down and out, unable to meet her obligations economically, politically, or militarily, and largely populated by long-haired lay-abouts and ne'er-do-wells. There was not much point in arguing about this because they had reached the stage of not believing a word any Britisher said. It seemed to me that if we could take out a boat and a crew who could beat them in their own waters, we might do something to change that depressing view of Britain. But it was quite an undertaking.

We began finding out all we could about the race. We then discovered that there was a series of four races in Sydney in December, the last of which was the Sydney–Hobart Race starting on the morning of Boxing Day, 26 December. These races were individual contests, but national teams and Australian State teams with three boats each could be entered for the Southern Cross Cup – the Pacific equivalent of the Admiral's Cup at home, though by no means so well recognized or so heavily contested. The races started in the middle of December, which meant having the boat out there in the first few days of the month at the latest. The crew would have to be there shortly afterwards so that they could get acclimatized. Going from the damp of an English December to the dry heat of Sydney is quite a change, especially when you have not been sailing for a couple of months. It takes a bit of time to get back into top form in those conditions.

The first problem was how to get the boat out to Australia. I thought it prudent to ask Teddy Denman, an old friend from school days who has always handled my insurance for me, to look around to see how this could be done, which ships were available and what it would cost. He came back to say that he had found a ship leaving early in October which could take *Morning Cloud* and he had made a provisional reservation on her. I then went off on an official visit to New Zealand where I was able to talk to some of the crew of Chris Bouzaid's boat *Rainbow* which had won the Sydney-Hobart Race the previous Christmas. On my way home I passed through Sydney and made contact with the sailing community there.

Meantime the Royal Ocean Racing Club had decided to send a team to compete in the Southern Cross series. They chose Max Aitken's *Crusade,* Arthur Slater's *Prospect of Whitby* and Rodney Hill's *Morning After,* our sister ship. Arthur Slater was appointed captain and we were invited to be reserve boat.

Throughout we were treated in every way like a member of the team and we were able to take advantage of the even more generous arrangements made by Qantas for ferrying the crews out and back. I also received a contribution towards the cost of shipping the boat. I had contracted to pay £750 for shipping *Morning Cloud,* skilfully negotiated by Teddy Denman. As team funds later provided £400, the net cost to me was £350.

Some difficulty was encountered in providing shipping for the three team boats. At one point it was hinted that a Soviet ship would be prepared to take all four boats for a small sum, or even without payment. In my political position I could not accept such an offer, quite apart from the fact that I had already made the necessary arrangements. In the event, the team boats were split up and arrived at various times in different ways. *Morning Cloud* had to be transhipped at Melbourne to get to Sydney, but she had the most time there to prepare. *Prospect of Whitby* and *Morning After* arrived later. Max Aitken sailed *Crusade* round to Sydney from Melbourne, taking part in a feeder race, and hitting a substantial rock on the way out of Melbourne Harbour as a result of taking on an Australian navigator. His rudder was knocked askew, but despite this he managed to make Sydney at the head of the fleet and win the race on corrected time as well.

Apart from getting the boat ready and shipped, my main preoccupation at this time was settling the crew. Owen Parker, who had had so much to do with tuning the boat, sailing her at Burnham and afterwards getting her ready for shipment, agreed to come as sailing master, in other words to organize the boat both at sea and in her berth. Anthony Churchill, who had navigated for me on that first race in the North Sea as well as at Burnham after he had finished racing on *Phantom* in the Admiral's Cup, was able to take time off from his journalism. Jean Berger, whose immense technical knowledge and power of analysis contributed so much to our think tank sessions about fitting out the boat, was able to get away for a spell from his machine tool business and came as helmsman. On the foredeck there was Duncan Kay, who had first joined *Morning Cloud* on the Solent, but who in fact came from the east coast and was a friend both of Anthony Churchill and of Jean Berger. I then needed another helmsman, particularly one with offshore experience, and I invited Sammy Sampson, a six-foot-four East Anglian farmer, highly respected throughout the ocean-racing world, to come with us. Using the justification that he needed to examine the fruit-growing activities of the Tasmanians, he accepted willingly. With myself we were six. All the others were specialists in their own field, whilst at the same time being admirable all-rounders. Each had tremendous experience of racing both inshore and offshore. They were also individually very strong characters. My job was to get them working together as a crew and to use all this experience, intelligence and strength to create a winning boat.

26 December 1969

Boxing Day, 26 December 1969, was a glorious day with the hot sun shining out of a bright blue sky. Sydney Harbour looked magnificent, a gentle breeze just ruffling the water. Eleven o'clock on Boxing Day is the traditional time for the start of the Sydney–Hobart Race, but long before that the mass of boats carrying spectators was beginning to muster all the way along the harbour from the starting line to the Heads, through which the competing boats had to pass out into the southern Pacific. On the balconies of the houses along the waterfront, looking over innumerable bays, people were grouping in parties to toast the boats as they went past. The sides of the hills were covered with people, as many as half a million some said, waiting with excitement for the long race to begin. It was a splendid, bustling, colourful scene, worthy of a great occasion.

After being driven down to *Morning Cloud* I said goodbye to the driver who had been looking after me for the previous ten days. As we gazed at the boats preparing for the race I said to him: 'How wonderful it all is. What confidence everyone seems to have here in Australia. Tell me, why is it?' To which this young man, who had a wife and family and who had been telling me he was in the process of buying a new home, replied, quite simply: 'Because, sir, out here we know that tomorrow will always be better than today.' What confidence! Six months later in June 1970 I led the Conservative Party into a General Election campaign with a manifesto entitled 'A Better Tomorrow'. Little did my Australian driver know that he was to be the inspiration for that campaign.

I had always known that it would not be possible for me to sail on *Morning Cloud* for all four races of the Southern Cross in Australia because Parliament was sitting well into December. When I arrived in Sydney the boats were on the last leg of the two-hundred-mile race. At the airport I immediately got into a small private plane which had been lent to me and flew off to find the fleet. By this time it was widely spread. But after flying low over a considerable area we spotted *Morning Cloud* heading for home, but not very well placed. It had taken the crew longer to get acclimatized than they had expected. They had also found the seas off Sydney difficult to handle.

I was more fortunate than I expected. In the first short race, *Morning After*, one of the three British boats, had become entangled with a New Zealand boat at one of the marks. It was decided to sail the race again, even though it meant having two short races in rapid succession. I was there for both of these. Fairly quickly we got used to the new conditions, no tides to worry about and a rather long heaving swell outside the harbour. In the second short race we had an exciting finish. As we came up towards the finishing line we gradually overtook a New South Wales one-tonner, *Boambillie*, much bigger than ourselves. With our floater spinnaker up on a close reach in a light breeze we finally

57

passed them only a short distance from the line. We were exuberant. As the Australians crossed the line they stood together on deck and cheered *Morning Cloud*. True sportsmanship. This put us all in fine fettle for the Sydney–Hobart Race.

The next few days were spent preparing her for the big race. I wanted her ready in every detail by Christmas Eve, no matter how late we worked on her. The only exception was to be the fresh meat and vegetables. Sammy Sampson was commissioned to bring these on board shortly before we left our moorings. There was no room for an ice-box down below and we knew that fresh food would not keep for very long in that heat.

By early evening on Christmas Eve *Morning Cloud* was ready to race thirty-six hours later. We knew we could have an enjoyable Christmas Day. We spent it at the home of Tryg Halvorsen, over-looking Sydney Harbour. Tryg, an Australian of Norwegian ex-traction, had himself won the Sydney–Hobart four times. Now he was going as navigator on *Apollo,* one of the big Australian boats. We ate our Christmas dinner with all the usual festivities. After spending the afternoon talking over the race, we had a cup of tea and went to take leave of our host. As I left, Tryg Halvorsen followed me to the door and said: 'I have been watching you racing out here and I think you might well pull this off. But you will only do it if you go right out early on and stay right out. Good luck.' And he was gone.

We looked in at the berths on the way back to our hotel just to make sure that *Morning Cloud* was untouched. The whole marina was an amazing bustle of activity. The crews of all the other boats appeared to be rushing around trying to get ready in time. Alan Bond's large new boat *Apollo* had only recently come into her berth. Seeing me on the pontoon he beckoned me aboard and invited me to have a look round. I went below to find joiners and carpenters still busy putting in the basic furnishings. On deck I commented on the size of the spinnaker poles and asked him how she went downwind. 'I don't know,' he said. 'We have not tried them yet. If the wind stays we will have to take her down the Sound in the morning and run up towards the starting line to find out.' There seemed to be chaos everywhere, but at the same time com-plete confidence that on the day it would be all right.

There was nothing more for us to do. We had a quiet dinner on Christmas evening, an early night, and a sound sleep. After a good breakfast, we went down to the boat.

The race was started from a frigate by the Australian Prime Minister John Gorton. Although there was a record entry of seventy-nine boats, of which we were the smallest, there was plenty of room to manoeuvre on the start line. What caused me some alarm looking ahead was to see some four thousand boats of the spectator fleet stretching right along the harbour, obviously ready to move in on us once we were under way. The start line itself was most effectively policed; not a launch was allowed near it. Spec-

tators were biding their time. The thought of tacking with seventy-eight other boats, surrounded by four thousand more of every size and kind filled with rumbustious Australians out for a jolly, made me wonder whether we would ever get out of the harbour without colliding with one of them or being hit by some enthusiast.

We made a good start, just a second to spare. We had long practised this operation and we were proud of our drill. I was at the helm, Anthony Churchill, the navigator, was doing the timing and checking our position in relation to the line; Owen Parker was looking after the tactical situation as a whole. In a small boat we were so near each other that it was possible to have very close coordination without anyone needing to raise his voice.

Morning Cloud running down to Hobart in the early stage of the race

Once over the line we were on the wind going down the harbour, tacking once or twice as we got near the Heads. The fleet of spectator boats turned out to be extraordinarily well disciplined. They were careful to keep out of our way, not to take our wind, and not to come immediately across our bows. It only needed a quick indication that we were about to tack for them to get out of the way altogether. Going through the Heads we could see tens of thousands of people massed on the hill slopes with a splendid view of the fleet as it departed.

Once through the Heads and in a true north-north-easterly wind we got the big spinnaker up and went out to sea. Quite soon we were away from the difficult slop at the entrance to the harbour and moving on a long ocean swell. The breeze strengthened to about 20 knots, the sun shone with an occasional white cloud in the sky, and we were happily on our way.

We had given a lot of thought as to whether or not we should stay fairly close to the coast or go right out to sea. The direct line from Sydney to Hobart, the rhumb line as it is called, runs between ten and twenty miles off the coast. It is, of course, the shortest route. On the other hand, we thought that by keeping in we might well lose the wind at night. By going out we should be taking a longer course, but we hoped we would also hold the wind better. More than that, we were in search of the 'set', or current, to help us on our way down the coast.

Quite early on we had heard about this 'set', but I was astonished when I reached Australia to find out how little precise information there seemed to be about it. I do not think our Australian friends and competitors were withholding the information from us; it was just that they could not really tell us from their own experience much about it. At first we understood that it ran south, but there were some who said that in certain conditions it ran north. This depended on the strength of the prevailing wind and for how long it had been blowing. As we had had north-easterlies and north-westerlies for some time, it seemed to us there was a good chance it would be flowing south. Most people we talked to thought that it was to be found roughly along the hundred-fathom line. This posed a certain problem for us because our depth meter went no deeper than fifty fathoms. We had to judge where the hundred-fathom line was by dead reckoning.

We were told of two other ways by which we could recognize the set. The temperature of the water, which was normally 69 degrees Fahrenheit at that time of the year, would be up to 72 degrees. For this purpose, many Australian boats carried a thermometer in some part of their hull which could easily be read. As we had nothing of this kind we attached a thermometer to a line and dipped it overboard regularly every half-hour. Secondly, bluebottles – little blue jelly-fish – could be seen floating in this warm water. If we succeeded in finding the set flowing south, we would be sailing with up to a 2-knot current which would improve our position enormously. So we sailed out to find the set.

Our search took us about sixty miles offshore. Our thermometer never rose much above 70 degrees and only occasionally did we see bluebottles, but once out there we were convinced that we had a powerful current behind us. This was confirmed by our navigator when he compared the plots he had worked out from his daily reckoning with the results of the sights from his astro-navigation. Indeed, we could never have stayed so far out from shore had we not had astro-navigation to help us. I was fortunate in having three members of the crew, Anthony Churchill, Sammy Sampson and Jean Berger, all capable of using the sextant and making a good job of it. This is really vital for the Sydney–Hobart Race.

There is only one radio station between Sydney and Hobart, that on the north-easterly point of Tasmania, and it is not particularly strong. It can be helpful as a check on either dead reckoning or astro-navigation, but there is no other radio station with which it can be used as a direction-finding instrument to provide a fix, or position. Boats with no one on board capable of astro-navigation would have to keep reasonably close to the coast to check their position.

Under the racing instructions all boats had to report their position three times a day, essentially for safety reasons should the weather get really rough, as it frequently does in the Sydney–Hobart Race. In the first race twenty-five years previously, in which there were only nine competitors, eight boats who hove to in a gale were not heard of for a long period. The only skipper who battled on was John Illingworth, who emerged as British victor. Since then the race has always gone to Australians, except for one occasion when the New Zealanders triumphed.

The radio control vessel moved down the course in the middle of the fleet. Calling over the names of seventy-nine boats in order and recording their positions took quite a time on each occasion, but it enabled us to plot our competitors' places on the chart, to see how well they were doing, and to judge the sort of conditions

Still running, but on the other tack, far out to sea. The only time I ever wore a hat sailing!

under which they were sailing. In this way we watched the battle of the giants which was going on close inshore between *Crusade* and *Apollo*. On occasions we suspected that information was being provided for tactical reasons so as to influence other boats. One position given by *Morning After* showed her to be further out to sea than we were in *Morning Cloud*. Was this, we wondered, a plot to get us still further away from the coast? We listened eagerly to the next reports only to hear with some relief that *Morning After* was safely back near the coast again. Useful and interesting information was also often passed with the navigation report. On the second day out one boat described seeing a small group of killer whales. Later on we were to see another group ourselves. We had heard many stories of the damage they can do to small boats, either intentionally by attacking, or by coming up under their keel and over-turning them. We watched them keenly and with some apprehension, but after half an hour or so they moved off in the other direction.

We could not help noticing that some of the larger boats were missing from the evening six o'clock reports. 'Ah!', we said to ourselves, 'it's cocktail time on *Crusade*. Think of the fun they must be having.' Reporting also had its humorous moments. On one occasion, after the navigator on *Prospect of Whitby* had given his position, the control boat commented: 'Thank you *Prospect of Whitby*. That puts you plumb over Alice Springs. I hope you enjoy the rabbit shooting there.' No doubt *Prospect*'s navigator wished he could have been spared this Australian wit.

In my view, this reporting system, extremely efficiently organized, should be introduced to other ocean races. It is, of course, a controversial matter. There is the overall expense of having a control boat moving all the time with the fleet. There is the individual expense of installing long-distance radio on each boat. However, if ocean racing is to be efficiently organized, this general cost ought to be met and I do not believe that the cost of a radio as a proportion of the cost of an ocean-racing boat is such as to deter any skipper from installing one. The other argument is more concerned with seamanship and the tactics of sailing. 'Why should we reveal our course and our tactics to our competitors?' asked many skippers. Indeed, there is much to be said for this point of view. Against it must be set the safety advantages and the fact that it makes the sport much more interesting both for those taking part and for those interested ashore. In Australia the positions of boats are broadcast over the radio after each reporting session so that the public at large can follow the contest closely. This in itself musters support for the sport. This reporting system is much better organized on a compulsory rather than a voluntary basis. Voluntary reporting is a safety precaution for those who take part in it. There is a disadvantage, however. Some boats' positions are given away to others who do not reveal their own. In Britain more thought needs to be given to this aspect of ocean racing.

Having got our spinnaker up we sped along at between 7 and 8 knots. At times *Morning Cloud* planed over the long waves, and to Owen Parker's excited cries of, 'This is a big one. Come along ole gal!' she reached 10 knots and then went off the clock. From time to time, after a long run, we gybed, keeping all the time the same distance out to sea.

We kept our big spinnaker up continuously for sixty-seven and a half hours, the longest run that any of us can ever have had. Then, towards breakfast time on the fourth day out, the wind gradually became lighter. We changed over to the floater spinnaker, but soon there was no breeze left to fill even that. It drooped woefully. We were becalmed. Now and again came a puff. The wind appeared to be moving round the compass. We tried a light headsail, but after a short time this light, fluky breeze backed and we made another attempt with the floater. Again, after a while, the puff disappeared and all around us was calm. Yet none of us had the feeling we had often experienced in the English Channel and in the Irish Sea during the Fastnet Race the previous August that the calm had come to stay for hours. We sensed that we were on the point of a drastic wind change. It worried us.

We had listened to the weather forecasts all the way down the coast. From Sydney onwards they had said that a strong wind might come in from the south. Recently our navigator had picked up the broadcasts from Tasmania. Those north of us were saying the wind would come in from the south-west. In Tasmania they were forecasting a blow from the south-east. Which was it to be? If it were to come in from the south-east it would suit us admirably. From our way-out position we could tack in towards Tasmania on the wind, and with a bit of luck we should finish up not far north of the entrance to the Derwent River on which Hobart stands. Meanwhile, other boats close inshore would be short-tacking right down the Tasmanian coast. If the wind were to come in from the south-west, the inshore boats would benefit. We would be faced with a long tack of twenty hours or more which would put us somewhere near the north-east tip of Tasmania, whilst the inshore boats would have got down to the river estuary. That would be the price we would have to pay for the advantages of having gone so far offshore.

We waited, and gradually the wind filled in. It seemed an interminable wait, but in fact it could not have lasted more than an hour and a half. Then from the Antarctic across the Tasman Sea came the gale.

Until then it had been one of the most enjoyable experiences of sailing we had ever had. The weather had been perfect. When not on watch we could lie, sunbathing, on the deck, but in the evenings it was pleasantly cool. With little heel on the boat while running, work in the galley was easy. We had got through our fresh food during the first two days and then moved on to tinned and packaged foodstuffs. Our small cabin was only some ten feet long,

and, at its widest point, nine feet across. But no one felt cramped and there were no wet clothes around the place to worry about.

Now, suddenly, everything changed.

The wind blew from the south-east. Thank heaven for that. If it held from that direction and we could keep the boat going through the heavy sea we ought to make reasonable time to the Tasmanian coast.

As the wind got up we changed our headsails and began to reef the main – the dial was registering 35–40 knots, gusting to more than 50. By this time we were down to our number five headsail, with mainsail reefed to its numbers, battling our way through a heavy sea. On deck the crew on watch were getting soaked from the waves breaking over the boat and with the spray. The clouds got lower, visibility became poor and, indeed, was reduced almost to zero as it began to rain or, rather, hail. Hailstones flew at our faces like bullets. And the cold – never before had I known such bitter cold. We were now nearly five hundred miles further south than Sydney. The light disappeared much earlier and soon it was dark.

Down below life was far from easy. Cooking in our small galley was almost impossible as we heeled so far to starboard – not that anyone much wanted to eat. Everyone's clothes were soaked. There was little room to get them out of the way. Then, to our alarm, we found water steadily mounting in the bilges until it was well over the cabin floor. Where was it coming from? We could find no obvious answer to the question. The hull still appeared sound enough. Had the keel bolts worked loose, letting in the water? And, if so, how secure was our keel? Or was the water seeping through from some other point?

We worked the pump, but it seemed to be ineffective. Was the heavy heel of the boat keeping the water in the bilges away from the hose? On inspection this seemed to be the case. There was only one answer. That was to bale and keep on baling as long as the storm lasted. I set to with one of the crew off watch, and we kept at it continuously. That presented its own problems. To get rid of the buckets of water we had to open the hatch over the companion-way. If we were unlucky enough to do so as a wave washed over the boat, more water came below, splashing over the bunks, the galley and the chart table. Soon everything below was as wet as on deck. Baling kept down the water in the cabin. The storm got worse. Both boat and crew were taking a heavy pounding.

We were working on our usual system of changing watch every four hours. Two of the crew were on each watch, and the navigator and myself were always available and joined them from time to time. At one stage in the race we did two hours ourselves so that each watch in turn could have a clear six hours' sleep. Now I decided to change the system again. The driving wind and bitter cold made conditions in the cockpit so bad that no helmsman could do a complete watch. His crew, huddled down beside him, was in a wretched position. I changed the helmsmen round so that they

Morning Cloud after the storm, taken by a small aircraft that came on us by chance and flew on

Sudden preparations for the
last gybe before the finishing
line at Hobart

did one hour on and three hours off. Even an hour in those conditions was almost unbearable. As an emergency system it worked, but it made other crew duties more difficult.

That night, after twelve hours of the storm, we came up to the Tasmanian coast at the Freycinet Peninsula. This was rather further north than I had hoped, but the crew thought we had done well. Then we had to beat down the coast until we could turn up the estuary into Storm Bay, a distance of some 60 miles.

The storm continued, but as dawn came it seemed slowly to be blowing itself out. We were able to get a larger headsail up. As the sea went down we appeared to take less water on board and the intervals between baling out *Morning Cloud* grew longer.

We could see the coast clearly. The landmark we were seeking is known colloquially as the Organ Pipes, a high rock formation dropping vertically down to the sea in hollow half-pipe-like formation. The wind comes over the top and siphons down with increasing speed. This was one of the things Tryg Halvorsen had warned us about on Christmas Day. 'Either keep right in close alongside', he said, 'or keep right out. If you do anything else you will risk being knocked flat by the wind coming down the Pipes.' There was no point in trying to get in under them. We decided to keep right out, and with the wind now from the south we came into Storm Bay. It was then that we heard we stood a chance of winning. The rest of the story I have already told.

When we crossed the finishing line, we had been at sea for a few minutes over four-and-a-quarter days. When this time had been corrected to allow for our handicap rating it amounted to three days, four hours, twenty-five minutes and fifty-seven seconds.

This put us fifty-one minutes, twenty-two seconds ahead of the next boat, Arthur Slater's *Prospect of Whitby*. Allowing that we probably sailed some 700 miles from Sydney to Hobart, this gave us just under four-and-a-half seconds a mile in hand over the whole race. Not much! A bad tack, a poor bit of drill, or a wrong decision in the navigation could easily have cost us this.

The hospitality in Tasmania was tremendous. Our hosts almost managed to prevent us from getting on with the task of getting the boat ready to ship her back to England. When we did dismantle her we found that the keel bolts had indeed worked slightly loose. We could just see daylight between the keel and the hull, but this did not explain the amount of water we had taken on board. It was only when we examined her again back home that we found the water had been coming in through the gutter round the top of the cockpit lockers. A slight modification and all was well. We also found that the clevis pin, a pin which passes through the forestay to hold it on to the bow of the boat, was bent like a crooked finger and had just held. Had it given way, the forestay would have gone and with it the mast.

The presentation of the trophies by the Governor in a packed City Hall was a great occasion. For *Morning Cloud* we received nine trophies, including a replica of the Sydney–Hobart trophy. All of this Qantas kindly flew home for us.

In a short speech Max Aitken said it was the most efficiently organized race in which he had ever taken part. With that we all agreed. In my few words I emphasized the favourable impact such a contest could have on Anglo-Australian relationships in particular, and on Commonwealth friendship in general. I felt that perhaps the Australians no longer regarded us as being quite such a decadent people after all. Alas, our success was not sufficient for the British to win the Southern Cross Cup as a team. If *Morning Cloud* had been in the team instead of the reserve boat, the cup would have been ours.

After these celebrations I flew off to Canberra to spend a day with John Gorton, the Australian Prime Minister, and his wife and family at their home. Then I flew on to Indonesia.

In Djakarta I had my first talks with the new President and the Foreign Minister. There was no doubt about the friendliness of the Government towards the British, the desire to see our firms re-established in Indonesia and the wish to put an end to the differences between Indonesia, Malaysia and Singapore. A year earlier I had spoken to the Press Club in Canberra, outlining the Conservative plans for a resumption of our role in the Far East should we be returned to power. The President had no objection to this from the Indonesian point of view; indeed he welcomed it as a contribution to the stability of the area.

For me this visit provided a new personal interest. It was in Djakarta that I started to collect Chinese porcelain and ceramics, in particular celadon. Both the then ambassador and the British

Following page: Trophies from winning the 25th Sydney-Hobart Race. In the centre is the Sydney-Hobart trophy itself, of which a replica is kept by the winner

Council representative were well-informed enthusiasts about this subject. In January 1970 Indonesia was only just beginning to be recognized as a repository of much Chinese craftsmanship, the result of being an export market for southern China for several hundred years. Two or three local collectors had been exploring some of the multitude of islands making up that country. There they found treasures still in everyday household use. Very often these were bought on a communal basis, the total payment being a small boat or some other item useful to the village community. Apart from a number of small celadon cups and jars, I was able to buy for just a few pounds a beautiful Swatow bowl (made about 1590), some nineteen inches across, which we carefully protected and brought home. A few months later, when I became Prime Minister, it rested on the table in the hall of my flat at 10 Downing Street. Every time I looked at it there seemed to me to be something particularly romantic about its story. Fashioned by some loving potter in southern China more than 350 years ago, it had then followed the pattern of trade to the Indonesian islands. There it was used by some family day in and day out until discovered by a dealer searching for treasures and brought back to the capital of the newly established independent country. From there it travelled half-way across the world by the most modern form of transport, finally to rest on the table of the Prime Minister of Britain. How could any potter have foreseen such a future for his bowl? Alas, in the move from 10 Downing Street to my home four years later it was smashed. I was heartbroken. And so ended the story of that precious Ming bowl.

In Singapore the Prime Minister, Lee Kuang Yew, was as stimulating as ever and anxious for me to see the tremendous developments which had taken place on the island since my last visit four years earlier. Massive new housing projects had been completed, large modern hotels had sprung up, and the vast industrial estate was well under way. It was all exciting, but it did not prevent me from driving out to my favourite haunt, the orchid farm to the north of the island. There you can not only see almost any variety of orchid growing in the open, you can also have them sent to your friends all over the world. You choose your blooms and in less than thirty-six hours they can be adorning a room in London.

My first visit to Hong Kong followed. If Singapore was exciting, Hong Kong was breathtaking. Never having given it much thought before, but having in my mind a picture of a somewhat barren rock rather like Gibraltar, with slums smothering new territory on the mainland, I was taken aback by the beauty of the setting, the splendour of the sky-line, the extent of the modern development, and the efficiency of the organization. Above all, I was impressed by the way in which more than two-and-a-half million refugees had been absorbed into the life of such a tiny entity, housed mostly in high flats provided for them, and their other needs

met. A visit to some of the few remaining slums on the side of a hill near the sea, with water trickling down through them, showed what still remained to be done. This cannot diminish the remarkable success which the island has already had. In the course of three days I was able to meet not only the various organizations concerned with the politics and administration of the island, but also a large number of individuals, many of whom have remained my friends. Nor must I forget the Hong Kong Yacht Club which gave me a most friendly welcome and always remained in touch with me. I was glad that in 1975 Hong Kong was able to enter a team in the Admiral's Cup races at Cowes.

In Hobart many had pressed me – apparently not attributing undue weight to my political responsibilities – to sail on *Morning Cloud* in the Hobart–Auckland Race which was starting early in January. 'Then,' they said, invitingly, 'you can take the boat to Hong Kong and race from Hong Kong to Manila in March.' This I was also urged to do in the Hong Kong Yacht Club. After Manila, it was suggested we could sail across the Pacific through the Panama Canal and take part in the Trans-Atlantic Race, arriving in England just in time for Cowes Week. To all these sailors this seemed a rather obvious and enjoyable season's racing. Work – and perhaps politics – is indeed the curse of the sailing classes!

And so we flew home just in time for the Boat Show. It was there, with the crew in the cockpit of the sister ship of *Morning Cloud,* that we did one of the best, and certainly one of the most enjoyable, television broadcasts in which I have ever taken part – *Sports Night with Coleman.* It must have been the first time that ocean racing had ever been put in such a high spot on television. Perhaps we were beginning to make an impact?

'Harold, you're cheating again!'

7 The Second Morning Cloud: The Admiral's Cup 1971

What were we to do next? For the 1970 season we obviously had to sail the first *Morning Cloud* again. She arrived back from Australia at Antwerp in March, and Owen Parker and some of the crew sailed her across to the Solent. There we raced with some success and a great deal of enjoyment until the end of August when we took her round to the east coast for Burnham Week. There we had even more fun sailing than usual. Rodney Hill was no longer sailing *Morning After,* our sister ship which had also been out in Australia, but had bought *Morningtown,* a bigger boat and the one-tonner after whom we were all named. It was not as satisfying racing against him in this way as our previous S&S 34 racing had been, but we found that normally we could hold him until the wind got above 15—18 knots. After that he roared away from us.

On Saturday at Burnham there is the major event of the week, the Town Cup. This is reserved for the bigger boats, a somewhat contentious matter for the rest of us. The town, however, insists on adhering to its point that the Town Cup is there to attract trade to the town and for that it needs the big boats. They must have this special inducement. For the rest of us there is the Commodore's Cup, lower in status and prestige, but usually sailed over the same course. On this occasion the most extraordinary incident occurred which I have never known repeated. What happened was this.

The big boats started first; we watched some of them go down-river some way beyond the starting line, then, turning round, they came in fast to starboard and when just back over the starting line were thrown over to port to get a fast start along the north bank of the river. The fact that some of them got their timing wrong and were over the start line too soon did not change our view that it was the best tactic to follow. We did an experimental run to get our own timing right and then went down-river ready to come back for the start. Our five-minute gun had gone, after which, of course, we were racing according to the rules. Anthony Churchill, who was navigating, had just shouted, 'A minute and a half to go!' when, inexplicably, two guns were fired. I was at the helm, thinking that we had just about got the timing right, when I was taken aback by this sudden intrusion. 'What the hell does that mean?' I shouted at Anthony, bearing away slightly as a reaction at the same time. 'Must mean a postponement,' was the first reply, followed rapidly by, 'It can't be. They'd have had to do it before the five–minute gun.' There was considerable confusion all around. 'We'll race on,' I shouted, and swung hard over to port, crossing the line a few seconds later, our perfect timing spoilt. 'Could be a change of course,' someone suggested. 'Well then, look quickly at the board,' I shouted at Anthony. 'Has it been changed? And get those sailing instructions up quickly.'

The course for the Town Cup and the Commodore's Cup is usually a longish one of some 36–38 miles out into the North Sea. One eagle–eyed member of the crew volunteered the information that the course was changed on the board before our starting gun. We checked the new letters with the sailing instructions to find that it provided only a short course a few miles outside the river mouth and then back home. 'That can't be right,' I said. 'Whatever the explanation we must be doing the long course.' 'What is more,' added Anthony, 'a course can't be changed after the five–minute gun.' 'That settles it,' I said. 'We'll sail the full course. We'd better stop arguing and get on with it. If the Race Committee has made a mistake and we are in the right, we can protest to them afterwards.'

By the time we had got to the mouth of the river we had settled down. *Morningtown,* going well in a breeze, was the only boat ahead of us. As we came up to the buoy which was the limit of the short course, we saw *Morningtown* getting her spinnaker ready. 'My God,' I said, 'she is going round that mark, putting her spinnaker up and doing the short course.' Once again the argument broke out and I told Anthony Churchill to have yet one

continued on page 109

The long procession up the River Crouch home to Burnham. First *Morning Cloud*, September 1970

Far right: Brittany in the
1950s. Vaurien dinghy

Right: Broadstairs, 1966.
Foreland class dinghy

Below right: With dinghy at
Broadstairs, August 1967

A Sailor's Album

From dinghy to ocean racer –
a record in colour

Rigging the Snipe at Broadstairs before racing, 1967

Right: The first ocean race. With Maurice Laing in 'Clarion of Wight' off Cowes at the start of the Cowes–Dinard Race, July 1968

The first 'Morning Cloud' in the Sydney–Hobart Race, 1969-70
Opposite: Second day out in the Sydney–Hobart Race. Below: In the gale on the third day out
(Painting by J. Beetham)

The first 'Morning Cloud'
End of Round the Island
Race, 1970

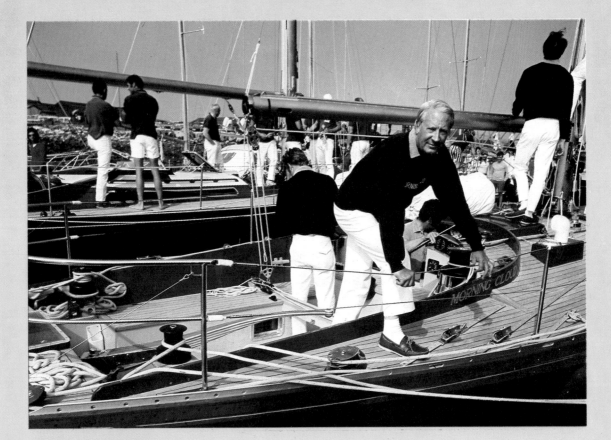

The second 'Morning Cloud' 1971
Opposite: Solent Points Race
Above: Cowes Week
Overleaf: The Wednesday of
the Admiral's Cup, 1971

At the helm on the Solent
during the Admiral's Cup.
Above: The victorious crew

The second 'Morning Cloud'. Above: Wednesday of the Admiral's Cup, 1971. Opposite: Sunset at Burnham

The second 'Morning Cloud'
At St Malo after the Cowes –
Dinard Race, 1971
Opposite: At Burnham.
'Vendetta' on right

The second 'Morning Cloud' during the Fastnet Race, 1971
(Deryck Foster, 1972)

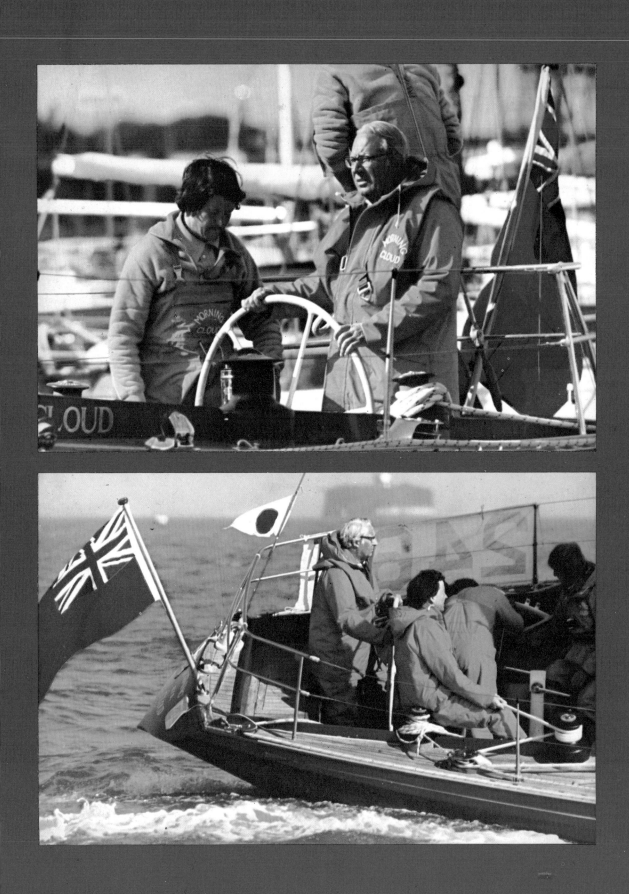

Admiral's Cup trials 1973.
Negotiating a buoy

Opposite:
The third 'Morning Cloud'
going into the Channel, 1973

The third 'Morning Cloud' off the Royal Yacht Squadron, Cowes
(Deryck Foster, 1974)

The fourth 'Morning Cloud'
Channel Race,
May, 1975
Overleaf: On board,
with author at the helm

The fourth 'Morning Cloud'. Above and overleaf: Solent Points Race

The first 'Morning Cloud'
Winner 25th Sydney–Hobart Race 1969

The second 'Morning Cloud'
British winning team, Admiral's Cup, 1971

The second 'Morning Cloud'
British Southern Cross Cup Team, 1971.
Winner 1B Division Sydney–Hobart Race, 1971.
Winner all seven races and Town Cup,
Burnham Week, 1972

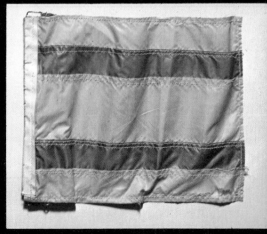

The third 'Morning Cloud'
British Admiral's Cup Team, 1973.
Winner Solent Points Championship, 1973

more look at the regulations. It was then that he came up with the answer that the two guns must have been a change of course for the next class after us, fired before their five-minute gun. That confirmed our view. We must sail on.

By this time Rodney Hill in *Morningtown* had rounded the mark, set his light-blue spinnaker perfectly and was sailing back towards us on his way up-river and home to a victory, as he thought. Quick as a flash Owen Parker shouted to Duncan Kay, on the foredeck, 'Get that spinnaker up from below quickly. Hurry!' Duncan leapt to it and I wondered what on earth he was going to do. Up he came with it in its container, the turtle. 'Walk along the deck with it as we go past *Morningtown*,' said Owen, and Duncan rather ostentatiously moved up into the bow. Rodney Hill at the helm of *Morningtown* smiled broadly as he went past. As soon as his back was turned the spinnaker was brought back again. We sailed on past the mark out on the long course. We were now watching carefully to see what the rest of the fleet would do. Would they turn and follow *Morningtown,* or would they follow us?

The boat behind us was a sister ship, *Ailish*, always well sailed and a keen competitor. We had seen at the start that this time she had one of the local boat-builders on board who knew everything there was to be known about racing on the River Crouch. 'Good Lord,' from Anthony Churchill, 'she is putting her spinnaker in the bow. Well, if they think it is the short course, we really have had it.' The crew watched even more anxiously. To our relief, as *Ailish* passed the mark her foredeck hand picked up the spinnaker and took it back aft. She had played the same trick on *Morningtown* as we had done.

Only one other boat followed *Ailish*. The rest turned at the mark, put up their spinnaker and sailed home almost in time for lunch. Three of us went round the long course. About four o'clock in the afternoon my navigator heard a plaintive voice on the police radio saying that practically the whole fleet had been back over the finishing line for some hours. Were we all right and when were we likely to get back home?

I told Anthony to reply rather tersely, 'In another hour or so, when we have finished the course.' An hour and a half later we sailed up the river flying our protest flag, ready to argue our case against the rest of the fleet. It was unnecessary. My security men came out in the launch to greet us, a smile of relief on their faces. 'It's all right,' one of them said, 'all of those in front of you have now retired from the race. They followed the wrong course.' There flicked back into my mind the memory of Rodney Hill saying to me the first time I went to Burnham, 'I know you are rather new to this game. The most important thing if you are racing up here at Burnham is to know the rules. If you take my advice you will get to know them inside out.' Good advice I thought, as I accepted that evening the Commodore's Cup.

In June 1970 a complete change in my circumstances took place. The Conservatives won the General Election and I became Prime Minister. It was immediately suggested that I should stop driving my own car, to which I agreed. It would have been pointless to have gone on driving. After the necessary means of communication had been installed in the car and a security man put in the front, there was not very much room for anything else. It was also suggested that I might wish to give up ocean racing because of the problems of security involved and the dangers to a

First *Morning Cloud* victories.
Below: after winning
the Commodore's Cup at
Burnham in 1970 (left to
right: Peter Dove, Anthony
Churchill, self, George Stead,
Owen Parker, Duncan Kay).
Right: The Ramsgate Gold
Cup, won in August 1970

Prime Minister. This I flatly refused to do. Two problems then arose. How should the necessary security precautions be taken while I was racing at sea? And, secondly, how could I be kept in immediate communication with 10 Downing Street in those circumstances? Everyone put their heads together and began to come up with solutions.

Communications were the least difficult. The equipment was available, but its weight was considerable. As we had done everything possible to pare off each unnecessary pound in the boat, it

First *Morning Cloud* heading for the finishing line at the end of the 'Round the Island' Race, 1970. The tiller is pulled so closely to me, not as a result of excessive weather helm, but because a pin in the stock had already sheared; but it lasted out the race

was something of a setback to have a double lot of radio equipment loaded on board. But it had to be accepted and the experts were most helpful in producing from time to time more light-weight equipment.

Effective security precautions were more difficult. The first suggestion was that I should always carry at least one, preferably two, security personnel on the boat. If it meant two extra men, I said, then it just was not on, and even if there were two available who were first-class sailors it would mean getting rid of two of my own existing crew, which was not on either. Next, what about a frigate to accompany us wherever we went? That, I said, was not going to be very good for public relations during our ventures; and what about the impact of its wash upon the rest of the ocean-racing fleet? Then a helicopter permanently overhead was proposed. All right, I replied, provided its wind disturbs our competitors but does not affect us; but would we be able to stand the noise for 220 miles of racing, which would not be very popular either?

In the end we reached a compromise. No close-up security precautions would be taken unless exceptional circumstances developed. In fact, these were provided for the Fastnet Race the following year, both by air and by sea. They were discreet and worked perfectly. As far as getting me back to No. 10 quickly was concerned, it was agreed that with first-class radio communications and a helicopter they could always come out to take me off the boat. Even this presented some difficulties and a moment of humour. The proposed drill was explained to me. After a radio communication a helicopter would come out and drop its ladder, down which would come a member of the crew. I would then be lashed with him to the ladder, which would thereupon be winched up into the helicopter. So far so good. 'But what is happening to *Morning Cloud* while all this is going on?' asked Owen Parker. 'Oh, I suppose she drops all her sails and heaves to while we carry out our operation,' was the reply. 'What, and lose precious minutes of racing time while you take the skipper off? Not on your life! If you want the skipper we'll push him off in a rubber dinghy and you can pick him up from there while we go on racing,' was Owen Parker's firm declaration. Fortunately, the need never arose, but the crew of *Morning Cloud* were determined to give priority to their racing.

We now started thinking about the future. Still the question was, what to do next? Let's go for the Admiral's Cup was the crew's rather obvious plea. The Admiral's Cup is more recently established than the America's Cup, a contest for twelve-metre boats fought out in the waters of Newport, Rhode Island, on the eastern seaboard of the United States. An American boat has won it on every occasion since the first contest more than a hundred years ago. There are qualifying rounds, but the contest proper is between only two boats. The Admiral's Cup was established only eighteen years ago, but it is already recognized as the foremost trophy in the ocean-racing world. Competition is between national teams, each of three boats, and the race is held every alternate year in British waters. The programme always consists of a Channel race of about 220 miles over the first weekend of Cowes Week, followed by two 30-mile races round the Solent on two separate days in Cowes Week itself, and finishing with the 605-mile Fastnet Race from Cowes to the Fastnet Rock in Southern Ireland and back to Plymouth. The short races receive a single point, the Channel double points, and Fastnet treble points. This is a testing programme for which between fifteen and twenty nations now send teams.

The first *Morning Cloud* was too small to be eligible for the British Admiral's Cup team. If we were to enter there would have to be a new boat. Uffa Fox, who had followed our fortunes closely, and who had always watched us from the balcony of his house overlooking the moorings at Cowes as we came in from racing, told me that in any case I ought to get a larger boat. If he saw anything wrong with the boat as we came in he always waved me up to hear his views, never sparing either the crew or the boat in the process. On one such an occasion he advised me to get something over forty feet in overall length, six feet longer than the first *Morning Cloud*. It was essential, he said, to deal with the south-westerlies coming across the Atlantic. 'And take my advice,' he added, 'get it built in wood and get it built by Clare Lallow next door.' It was sound advice, but we had to get down to the details.

The think-tank sessions continued, but they were now moved from my flat in Albany, Piccadilly, to Chequers, and usually took place on a Sunday evening. After I had sailed and cleared the Red Boxes of state papers, we were able to spend a couple of hours with a bite of food working out what we wanted.

About this time an American friend sent me a copy of a book called *Defending the America's Cup*. It contained the whole story of *Intrepid's* triumph, from the moment the thought occurred to the leader of the successful syndicate that he might get an organization to back a boat for the attempt, to the moment of victory when the crew were thrown in traditional manner into the sea. I was fascinated by it. It detailed conversations between the leader and his colleagues on the syndicate about the best way to raise the necessary money, the discussions with Olin Stephens on the design of the boat, and the effort, finally successful, to persuade Bus Mosbacher to steer it. The details of the equipment were all there, together with the teething troubles encountered in getting the boat tuned up. Perhaps the most interesting of all were the discussions about the make-up of the crew, how Mosbacher picked them, handled them during their long training periods, maintained their morale, and finally turned them into the successful contender. I learnt much from that book. Later, when he was in charge of protocol at the White House, Bus was to present me with his own autographed copy of it.

With all this in mind we decided that the new *Morning Cloud* must be a racing machine. Everything must be directed to that end. Anything unnecessary must be sacrificed. I asked Olin Stephens to prepare some designs, telling him what we wanted. We had in mind an Admiral's Cup boat round about 40–41 feet overall, with a lay-out on deck and below deck which we had been working on. In particular, we wanted a flush deck – in other words, one that was flat, or almost flat, without the usual projections of a coach-roof. This requirement posed problems of getting sufficient head-room down below, as well as enough light, there being neither portholes nor windows hitherto customary in the coach roofs to let the light through. Olin agreed that if it could be managed, it would be a stronger construction than the normal deck type. We had also worked out a cockpit to which we brought back almost all the winches so that they could be worked easily by the crew stand-ing there, rather than on the deck up by the mast. This we discussed in great detail with Rod Stephens, who once again showed his uncanny flair for being able to think through each proposal clearly, to see any snags there might be, and often to improve upon it in the process.

We had also been doing a lot of thinking about the winches. We knew it would be a great help on a bigger boat if we could work the winches on each side of the boat together. This meant they would have to be connected in some way or other, and, of course, able to be disconnected when required. Two of the members of the crew were associated with a firm who provided our winches for the first *Morning Cloud* and who were doing so again for the second. They agreed to do the development work for interconnected winches of

Receiving the half-model of the first *Morning Cloud* at the Boat Show, 1971. Olin Stephens, the designer, stands on my right

the kind we described, provided I covered the cost, in exchange for which I had the exclusive right to use the winches in the Admiral's Cup year. These winches proved to be highly successful and the envy of many another boat. First there were two-speed winches, which have led, with our encouragement, to three-speed winches, interconnected, and now to a three-speed interconnected pedestal winch for the cockpit of the fourth *Morning Cloud*. On this boat we also have the first self-tailing winch for the mainsheet, produced by a British firm. Here is an example of the successful products of close teamwork between an ocean-racing crew and the equipment manufacturer. We have benefited, other boats have followed suit, and the nation has gained exports from the world-wide knowledge of what these successful projects have done for us on successive *Morning Clouds*.

Building the second *Morning Cloud*. Below: Polishing the topsides of the hull in Clare Lallow's yard. Right: The mast step section made of stainless steel

Below deck we wanted the minimum necessary for racing. Aft, the navigator's cabin on the port side was designed by Anthony Churchill. The galley opposite was small and easily manageable in the worst weather. We paid great attention to the detail of the lockers for storing foodstuffs. Midships we had a tier of three single bunks for each side of the boat, and forward of the mast was reserved for sail storage in canvas bins with a light aluminium rail round the top. Right up in the fore peak we put the heads with a small canvas curtain which could be pulled across. Next to the Blake toilet was a small hand wash-basin. While she was being constructed the builder told me he wished to raise a rather delicate problem. The crew had told him that they could save weight up for'ard by not having a wash-basin; and, in any case, it really was not necessary to wash at sea. On the other hand, he, the builder,

thought I might wish to use it occasionally and he had therefore found a very light-weight basin which he could install. What was the decision to be? I opted for the basin.

I naturally consulted Olin Stephens about a boat builder. If I wanted it in aluminium alloy, he told me, it was probably best to get it built in Holland. British builders in alloy had not had much experience of building ocean-racing boats in this material. It was obviously not possible for me to go to Holland. I could just about get away with an American designer, though this produced one or two angry outbursts from their English competitors, but the boat itself and most of its equipment would obviously have to be British. For a boat in wood, said Olin Stephens, I could not do better than to go to Clare Lallow, thus offering me the same advice as Uffa Fox. There is a remarkable intuitive understanding between Clare and Olin which obviates the need for the usual mass of detailed design drawings which are required by most builders. Clare Lallow has built so many Sparkman and Stephens boats that the merest indication of the design is immediately translated

Above: The three boats in the British Southern Cross Cup team, *Morning Cloud, Cervantes IV* and *Prospect of Whitby,* awaiting loading at Liverpool for Australia, October 1971. Right: *Morning Cloud* is loaded

by Clare into practical reality. Clare Lallow agreed to build the second *Morning Cloud,* and fortunately had well-seasoned timber available for her.

That autumn I went as Prime Minister to the Special Assembly of the United Nations to celebrate the twenty-fifth anniversary of its foundation. This gave me the opportunity of spending a couple of afternoons in Olin Stephens' office. On this occasion I went with a list of points, rather longer than the twenty-four produced by Rod on the first *Morning Cloud,* which had been agreed by all the crew in Britain. By the time I left, practically all the points about the boat had been settled; the designs were then sent to Clare Lallow and building began. From time to time during the winter we made a point of going down together to his yard to see how the construction was getting on. It gave the whole crew the chance mentally to record everything about the boat, so that if in future anything went wrong they would know where to look for the trouble and what to do about it. It also gave us complete confidence in her. We then turned to our plans for the racing season.

The second *Morning Cloud* was launched on 10 April 1971. This time the bottle of champagne, again from the hands of my stepmother, did its job the first time. There, sliding down the slip, was the racing machine on which we had set out hearts. Yet how beautiful she looked as she entered the water. Some of the experts commented that, with her rather shallow shape of hull underwater, she would be splendid downwind, but not much of a performer on the wind. They were to be totally confounded.

We took her out on trials as soon as we could, directly after lunch. Perhaps it was too soon. The boat had not been in the water long enough to settle down and let the sea use its influence on it. Whether or not this was the case, we found ourselves in difficulty when a leak occurred after we had been out for an hour or so. It was traced to the garbords in the bottom of the hull where the strain on the planking had opened up a very small gap. With further strengthening under Rod Stephens' supervision some ten days later this was quickly put right. All the crew had set aside Easter week after the launching so that we could tune the boat, and get used to handling her and working together as a crew.

Champagne at the launching
of the second *Morning Cloud*,
April 1971. Below: Splashed
in the traditional way over
the bows by my stepmother,
and (right), toasting the
success of the new boat with
Sir Alec Rose, the round-
the-world yachtsman

Below right: Second
Morning Cloud in berth at
Port Hamble, May 1971

Following pages: Second
Morning Cloud in her first
race round the Solent, May
1971

We had expanded from six to eight in order to handle the larger boat, and a week's continuous sailing together gave us the chance of getting used to handling the heavier equipment and also of working out and practising our drills. For this purpose eight days' continuous sailing is worth infinitely more than eight separate days at weekends. When racing began we felt the full benefit of this training period. *Morning Cloud* had been launched in good time and we were very confident when the Admiral's Cup trials began.

The trials took place in June and consisted of two weekends of Channel races and two weekends of short races around the Solent. When the team was chosen we were delighted to find ourselves included, together with *Cervantes IV,* roughly the same size as ourselves, and *Prospect of Whitby,* a larger boat. *Quailo,* a fifty-five-foot boat built by Camper and Nicholson, was the reserve boat. I accepted an invitation to captain the team, the only occasion on which a British Prime Minister has skippered a British team in an international sporting event.

To be captain of such a team posed a number of questions. What in fact could the captain do? Obviously he could try to ensure that the team had all the resources they needed, but even this was very largely the responsibility of the owners, who certainly did not want anyone else interfering in their affairs. There were certain communal facilities which we were able to arrange, such as special meteorological briefing for the Channel races and the Fastnet. But once out on the ocean, each boat was on its own. There was nothing a team captain could do about it.

To me it seemed that the most valuable thing I could do would be to make sure the morale of the team was as high as possible. I expanded the *Morning Cloud* think-tank to include the whole team. One glorious July Sunday evening all the members of the team, including that of the reserve boat, came out to Chequers. There we got to know each other better, sat round exchanging information and ideas, not only about out own boats, but about our competitors, and also talked about tactics on the Solent. All this sounds straightforward and rather obvious, but it was the first time it had happened. It did much to create a team spirit which proved its worth later in the first short race on the Solent.

All British teams in the Admiral's Cup face one major problem, to which no solution has ever been found. Under the rules, the national teams have to be nominated by 30 June, and as a result the trials have to be completed by that date. Until then every crew concentrates its utmost on getting into the team. The competition is fierce – there were twenty-eight boats trying for a place in 1971 – the tension mounting until it reaches its peak during the last weekend. At that point most of the boats are probably at the height of their efficiency. Once the team has been announced the tension drops. On other boats crews that have worked together for several months begin to disintegrate, and there is nothing left but the option of individual racing and the social joys of Cowes Week, if that is what they like. But this also affects crews chosen for the team, who suddenly find that the intense concentration demanded by the trials has eased. Once their first objective has been achieved there is not the same atmosphere about the intervening races before the Admiral's Cup Race begins. Everywhere there is an air of anticlimax. It is probably true to say that no team can be kept at the same level of intensity after the last trial and until the Cup races proper begin. A relaxation in

Left: Second *Morning Cloud* hard on the wind off Cowes, 1971. Self on tiller

Below: *Morning Cloud* with her spinnaker up

The British Admiral's Cup team making practice starts, July 1971. Left to right: *Cervantes IV, Prospect of Whitby* and second *Morning Cloud*

effort has to be expected. The problem is how to get the team keyed up again to make their maximum effort when they face the international competition. This is made all the more difficult because relaxation and regeneration have both to take place in the short period of one month. I talked this over with Roger Bannister, a doctor as well as a world-famous athlete, and he agreed about the immense difficulty of arranging any sailing programme which could cope with this situation.

Other international teams face no such intractable problems. Nor, for that matter, does a British team when it goes abroad to race. Countries overseas choose their teams long before the final date, if only because they have to have the time to ship their boats to Britain, arriving here some weeks before the Admiral's Cup Race begins. With boats and crews complete, they can sail every day, re-tune their boats, re-train their crews, and gradually work up to a peak by the time of the first Admiral's Cup race. Of course the problem could be solved for the British if the trials were concluded during the weekend before the Cup races begin. This would mean a change in the rules, which were deliberately drawn up so as not to give the British an advantage over other international competitors. As it turns out, this provision acts very much to our disadvantage. I thought a great deal about it, as indeed did Robin Aisher when he became skipper of the Admiral's Cup team two years later. It seemed to me the only thing I could do was to maintain the interest of the chosen crews as fully as possible and keep their spirits high as I have already described. Robin Aisher went further and introduced practice starts on the Squadron line at Cowes for the boats chosen. In part this has the same purpose, but it is difficult to convince oneself that four or five boats manoeuvring for the start line are really simulating the conditions they will have to face when anything between sixty and eighty competitors are fighting for positions on the line.

Now for the Admiral's Cup races themselves. The British team did well in the Channel Race, largely sailed on the wind in a good breeze. Of the Admiral's Cup boats, *Prospect of Whitby* was first, *Morning Cloud* third, and *Cervantes* fourth. Our team emerged with 270 points, a lead of thirty-six over the Americans and fifty-four over the Australians. There were twelve other national teams on the scorecard. In this high-spirited atmosphere lapel buttons appeared for the first time on the waterfront: 'Slater is Greater' boosted Arthur Slater, skipper of *Prospect of Whitby,* to be followed by 'Ted's Ahead' from the *Morning Cloud* supporters. The craze spread rapidly.

The first short race of the series was held on the Monday of Cowes Week. Parliament was still sitting. The previous Thursday the Labour Opposition had succeeded in obtaining an emergency debate on the ship-building situation on the Clyde for Monday afternoon. Having established his claim, Harold Wilson, Leader of the Labour Party, did not disguise his glee in demanding that I

should be present throughout the debate. Of course the House of Commons took priority. That went without saying. I was in my place on the front bench while *Morning Cloud* and the team were racing. I returned to Cowes that evening to find an aura of gloom. Our lead over the Americans had diminished to nine points, and over the Australians to thirty-seven. Although *Prospect of Whitby* had been second and *Morning Cloud* fourth, there had been a protest against *Cervantes* at the start and she had been disqualified. Bob Watson, her skipper, and his crew were dispirited and dejected. Then it was that our team meetings stood us in good stead and together we were able to restore their morale.

On the second short race on Wednesday there was a hard blow with gusts of over 35 knots. On the leg downwind, boats were broaching wildly all over the Solent, or so it seemed to us. On *Morning Cloud* we were using a spanker made by Ted Hood as a form of storm spinnaker. The strain on the boat was tremendous. Suddenly, as we were roaring back from the west Solent, we heard a loud crack of tearing wood. A winch normally used for a spinnaker sheet, but carrying a guy, came away from its mounting. It pinned Owen Parker against the rail, smashing into his arm, hand and thigh. Fortunately nothing was broken, but he was in acute pain for the rest of that race and suffered a great deal during the Fastnet. As a result of that race, the Australians moved up into second place, but we British had a lead of twenty-two points over them. Everything now depended on the result in the Fastnet.

On the Saturday morning we went down the Solent and through the Needles with a strong breeze. As we moved along the south coast we hit periods of calm. The wind seemed to be moving in lines, with calms interspersed. Round the Fastnet Rock we began the long run home with a really strong breeze and quite a big sea. Our big spinnaker up, *Morning Cloud* was showing, as usual, how difficult she was to control when running downwind. At times two men had to be on the tiller. They both needed to be tall so that they could put their feet on the opposite side of the cockpit and exert the necessary pressure. I had difficulty in doing this. I came to the conclusion that a forty-foot boat is just about the biggest you can handle with a tiller, and I began to think seriously of changing over to a wheel for the following season. At this juncture I thought *Morning Cloud* was over-pressed and I had an instinctive feeling that something would go unless we made a change. Although the crew were not happy about it, we came down to our spanker, but later, when the wind seemed to have lightened a few knots, back up went the spinnaker. It was then, halfway across the Irish Sea, that misfortune struck. I was below at the time; a loud crack, the boat shuddered, the violent rolling from side to side eased off and we seemed to be gently moving with the waves. Up on deck I found that the cups holding the spinnaker poles had been torn out of their tracks on the mast and could not be repaired. This, I thought, can lose *Morning Cloud* a place and the British the

Morning Cloud and her crew photographed before the start of the Channel Race, one of the races in the Admiral's Cup, in July 1971. Left to right: Duncan Kay, Owen Parker, Jean Berger, Sammy Sampson, Anthony Churchill, self, Peter Holt and Peter Dove

Second *Morning Cloud* in the Admiral's Cup, 1971. Left: Short tacking close inshore and (below) with mainsail reefed in the second short race in the Solent

Following pages: So near and yet so far. Short tacking in the second short race. We missed her. We had to – we were on port and *Levantades*, an Italian boat, is on starboard!

Admiral's Cup. Everyone was now on deck and the crew began to improvise. They quickly got a large headsail up and used a spinnaker pole hooked into an eye on the side of the mast to keep the sail well out. Then we began to think how we could rig a temporary arrangement to the spinnaker itself. The wind was getting lighter all the time and we knew that if we were to keep up any sort of speed at all we would have to fly the big spinnaker. Eventually, with a Heath-Robinson contraption, we hoisted the big spinnaker again with the pole similarly secured. The trouble was that the pole could hardly be adjusted at all. The outer end could be raised a little, but the inner end was securely fixed to the eye. When we had to gybe near the Scillies it took us nearly half an hour to move the pole from one side of the mast to the other. Meanwhile, unbeknown to us, though not far away, *Koomooloo,* one of the Australian team, had lost her rudder. To cap it all, round the Scillies we almost became becalmed. We struggled on.

Later, as the wind came in again, we felt hopeful. Nearing Plymouth, press boats came out to tell us the news. *Cervantes* had done well, making up for her incident in the first short race. At one stage she had looked like winning the race overall. In fact she was third, but she had won her class. With this great advantage Britain could still win the Cup. As *Morning Cloud* entered Plymouth Sound we were greeted with a bevy of boats all agog to see if we could make it in time to get the necessary points. It is not often, I supposed, that a Prime Minister sails home in this way. The Navy took full advantage of it. A frigate appeared on the horizon as we came along, and now the Admiral's launch took over as we sailed towards the finishing line. Marine commandos were in their rubber boats not far off, helping to keep some of the spectators far enough away to enable us to keep our wind. It was a great scene which took my mind back to the Sydney–Hobart Race.

We made it in time. *Prospect of Whitby* had got in ahead of us and all the pundits had done their calculations. The result – Britain regained the Admiral's Cup with 825 points and a lead of 43 over the Americans and 106 over the Australians, though they had the satisfaction of winning the race overall with *Ragamuffin,* skippered by Syd Fischer. 'Rago's Arse Beats Class' appeared at Plymouth – the last of the lapel buttons!

Once again *Morning Cloud* was greeted by cheering crowds on the dock. It was a moving moment for me to have captained the British team which regained the foremost racing trophy in the world. But Government business called. I left at once for 10 Downing Street, returning on Friday for the presentation of the Cup and the awards. From the Queen and Prince Philip on Britannia bound for the west coast of Scotland came a message of congratulations, and from the Prince of Wales a robust personal letter in his own hand. The American captain wrote that we deserved to win. It was a great triumph for Britain. I was glad to have played my part.

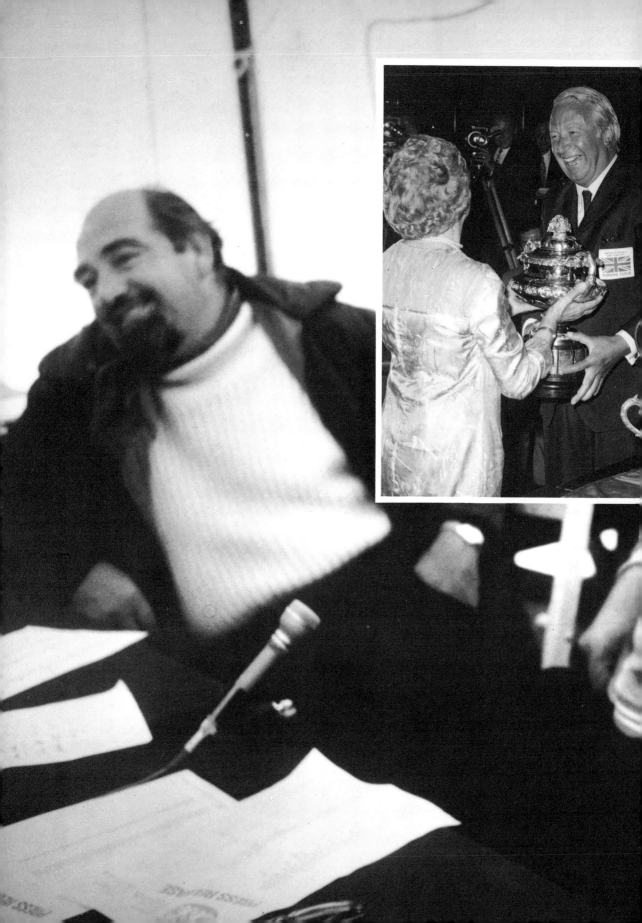

Plymouth, August 1971.
Press conference with (left)
Arthur Slater and (right)
Bob Watson. Inset:
Receiving the Admiral's
Cup as captain of the British
team from Mrs Aisher, wife
of the Admiral of the
R.O.R.C., Owen Aisher

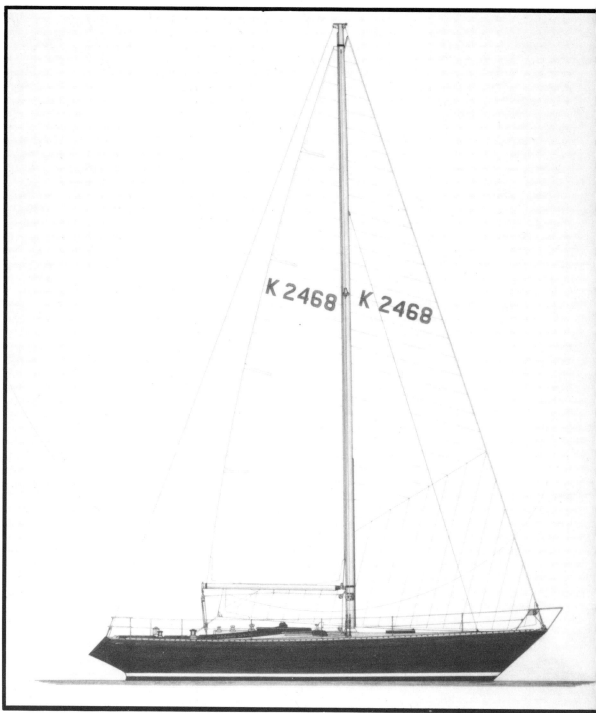

Morning Cloud

Scale drawings of the third
Morning Cloud, **1973**
(opposite) and fourth
Morning Cloud, **1975 (left)**

Second *Morning Cloud* short tacking on the River Crouch, Burnham Week, 1972

After our success in the Admiral's Cup I was invited to send the second *Morning Cloud* to Australia for the Southern Cross Cup series, this time as a member of the team. The crew were delighted at the thought of being able to compete again in the Sydney–Hobart Race. I knew that as Prime Minister it was highly unlikely that I would be able to get away for any of the races, but I was very glad for *Morning Cloud* to go. Before she was shipped we had fitted in a weekend's racing at Ramsgate and then our customary Burnham Week at the end of August. On each occasion we added to our victories. Perhaps the one we prized most was winning the Gold Roman Bowl as the overall victor in the 'Round the Island' Race. It proved to be the first of three successive wins, a feat never achieved before, though Max Aitken won it twice in succession, and difficult to achieve in the future.

Out in Australia, the crew, skippered by Sammy Sampson, almost brought about the double of winning the Sydney–Hobart Race again. On this occasion Anthony Churchill kept closer in to the coast and they were heading for victory when, some forty miles away from the estuary, they fell into a hole. It was infuriating for them to have to stand by and watch the New Zealand one-tonners bringing up the breeze behind them, demolishing their chances of success. Nevertheless, *Morning Cloud* won her class and the crew came to celebrate at No. 10 and to tell me the tales of their battles in the Pacific. After *Morning Cloud* had been shipped back, the tiller was replaced by a wheel. At first it seemed strange to me. That personal contact between the man steering the boat and the water, transmitted through the tiller to the rudder, disappeared. The touch of the dinghy sailor was lost. A new feel and a new technique had to be developed. There was no doubt, however, that *Morning Cloud* was easier to control with a wheel.

A season without the Admiral's Cup is always bound to be quiet and something of an anticlimax, but we put it to good use. Some of the crew went off to try a few races on other boats and to see whether there were any new ideas to be picked up. At the same time we tried out new crew on *Morning Cloud*. We certainly enjoyed the Solent, raced again at Ramsgate, and then went on to sweep the board at Burnham. This year the Royal Temple at Ramsgate and the Royal Burnham arranged jointly a race for the Trafalgar Bowl between the two ports across the Thames Estuary as a prelude to Burnham Week. It proved to be an inordinately long and difficult race, getting us into Burnham well after two o'clock in the morning. That we won. On the succeeding seven days' racing at Burnham we won on each occasion, culminating in the Town Cup. Eight victories in a row. Never before had every race in Burnham Week been won by a big boat.

These were our final successes with the second *Morning Cloud,* for already our think tank had been working on a new boat for the Admiral's Cup in 1973. Above all, we wanted one in which we could win the Fastnet. I told Olin Stephens of this and in particular of my view that as the Fastnet is usually a heavy-weather race, he should design us a boat for these sorts of conditions. This he did. It was ironical that the Fastnet in 1973 turned out to be a light-weather race, with many calm spells, and that a year later the third *Morning Cloud* was lost in a gale off the south coast of England.

We followed our usual procedures. As a crew we worked out the improvements we wanted to make from our experiences in the second *Morning Cloud*. The third was to be slightly bigger, forty-five feet overall, and the cockpit aft was to be extended into a double cockpit with still further concentration of the winches around the extension. Once again she was built by Clare Lallow, and we followed her construction with the same interest. She was built of three skins of mahogany, one on top of the other, at different angles, giving her great strength. This required that an even temperature should be maintained while the lengthy process of gluing the planking together was completed. To achieve this Clare Lallow constructed a large tent inside the yard, inside which the third *Morning Cloud* was built. This led to a stupid story circulating that a new secret design had been developed, enshrouded in mystery, which was being sternly guarded in the yard. One day a journalist walked into Clare Lallow's office, accompanied by photographers with all their equipment, and asked Clare where they could get the best view of the new boat in order to take photographs of it. 'Follow me', said Clare, 'and I'll show you.' He walked them back through the yard, out on to the pavement and across the road, and stopped by the entrance to his local pub. 'Now, gentlemen,' he said, 'you stand here and you will get the best picture you can of Mr Heath's boat in my yard. I'm going in to have my pint.' And that was that.

At the launching on 14 April 1973 an unhappy incident occurred. In the crush of people on the wall alongside the slipway the wife of one of my crew lost her balance and fell on to the concrete below, just as *Morning Cloud* had passed. Suffering badly from concussion, she was rushed off to hospital. 'This will be an unlucky boat', I heard someone nearby mutter.

We prepared ourselves in the same way for the Admiral's Cup trials and again we were selected. An informal inquiry was made whether I would captain the team again, if invited, but I declined, knowing that my responsibilities as Prime Minister would interfere with my duties as captain. In particular, the Commonwealth Prime Ministers' Conference was due to be held in Ottawa at the end of July and beginning of August, and it would obviously overlap into Cowes Week. I therefore missed the first three races of the Admiral's Cup. Having completed my discussions on the communiqué with my fellow Prime Ministers, I flew back from Ottawa overnight, arriving in Cowes on Friday morning in time to take part in the preparations for the Fastnet which began the next day. It proved to be the most frustrating

Third *Morning Cloud* (right) off the Needles in the 1973 'Round the Island' Race. She was to go on to win the race, the third time in succession for a *Morning Cloud*

ocean race in which I have so far taken part. It was without incident except for the fact that we were constantly becalmed. Coming back along the south coast of England we constantly sought a breeze by going inshore, but on each occasion, after raising our hopes, the breeze just died away. Those who stood out offshore got a breeze which carried them through. The Germans emerged for the first time as the victors. The monopoly of the British, Australians and Americans was broken. The only compensation for us on *Morning Cloud* was that we had won the 'Round the Island' Race for the third time running, and we proved to be the winner of the Solent points series over the whole season. We were invited to go to Australia again, but I declined. I knew it would be impossible for me to be out there for any of the races, and on this occasion I felt I did not want to be separated from the boat.

In February 1974 the Conservative Party lost the General Election and I became once again Leader of the Opposition. Although we obtained more votes than any other Party, we were in a minority of three in the House of Commons. It was obvious a further General Election could not be long delayed. Amidst all the uncertainty there was little time for sailing. In the second half of Cowes Week *Morning Cloud* swept the board. Light winds prevailed during the first three days of the week, then the blow began on Thursday. We won for the first time the New York Yacht Club Cup, one of the two main trophies of Cowes Week. On Friday we won the traditional Rocking-chair – for the second time – and on Saturday we were again successful. *Morning Cloud* was then taken round to Ramsgate.

There we won the 'Round the Goodwins' Race, some fifty miles from Ramsgate up the Thames Estuary, round the North, East, and South Goodwins and back home. It was a strange race. We did well round the Tonge Lightship in the Thames Estuary, with only two bigger boats ahead of us. Then, halfway to the North Goodwin Lightvessel, the wind faltered. We kedged. The rest of the fleet, including all the little boats, caught up, but were then swept inshore off the North Foreland, where they picked up a breeze which brought them out to the North Goodwin in front of us. When the breeze reached us – and this time it was about 20 knots – the race began all over again but this time we were at the back of the fleet. We worked hard and by the time we got out to the South Goodwin only two smaller boats were still in front of us.

Along Sandwich Bay a sudden storm struck. Fortunately, I saw it hit a cruising boat inshore first, and we got our big spinnaker down in time. We had then to make our way up the coast again before turning for Ramsgate. After the storm came the calm. The wind died away, but with just enough tide helping us we scraped round the last buoy, set our light starcut spinnaker and, holding our breath, aimed just north of Ramsgate harbour.

Third *Morning Cloud* along
the north shore on the heels
of *Battlecry*, but *Battlecry*
won the Britannia Cup on
the Tuesday of Cowes Week,
1974. Two days later, the
roles were reversed when,
after a long battle in a stiff
breeze, *Morning Cloud* beat
her to win the New York
Yacht Club trophy

Burnham Week 1974

Good sailing in Burnham
Week, 1974. Previous pages:
Out in the North Sea from
the Crouch (left to right:
Terry Leahy, Tubby Lee,
self, Duncan Kay). Above:
concentration. One of the
afterguard shouts at the
foredeck. Right: *Morning
Cloud* holds *Loujaine* (1971
Prospect of Whitby), steered
by Sir Maurice Laing

The end of the day. Above:
running up the Crouch to
our moorings (right)

Looking back we could see that everyone else was now having to battle their way against the tide with barely enough wind to help them over it. We crossed the finishing line and won by an hour and five minutes. Not bad for a heavy-weather boat.

We enjoyed Burnham Week, as always, but our successes were mixed. For the first time for five years we did not carry off any of the major trophies. But as usual we had a happy and enjoyable time. On the first Sunday we went on our traditional picnic to Paglesham, and on Saturday I was able to congratulate Maurice Laing on winning the Town Cup.

Early on the Sunday morning I left by air from Southend Airport for Ostend. I was going to join my former regimental comrades in Antwerp to celebrate the thirtieth anniversary of the liberation of the city in which my regiment had taken part.

Before I left Burnham I arranged for our 'movement crew' to take the boat from Burnham round the south coast to Cowes. The racing crew went back to their homes and their jobs. The 'movement crew' consists of experienced sailors, most of them also trained navigators, who have no boats of their own but who enjoy taking a few days off from their work to find the time to sail other people's boats from one racing centre to another. Our 'movement crew' had been doing this for me with all the *Morning Clouds,* but on this occasion my godson, Christopher Chadd, who had been down with his family, asked whether he could sail with *Morning Cloud* and I agreed. He, too, was an experienced sailor; he was fascinated by the boat and wanted to help sail her.

I flew back from Antwerp to London that same Sunday evening. On Monday there were reports of storms and rough seas off the south coast. At once *Morning Cloud* came into my mind, but I had every confidence in the boat and the movement crew. She was a heavy-weather boat and I knew that if the skipper had any doubts about the weather he would put in either to Ramsgate or to Dover; there were several days left in which to get her round to Hamble. I thought that the chances were that he would be going through the rough weather and into Southampton Water. On Tuesday morning, 3 September, just as I was having breakfast, I was telephoned by the police who said that they had just heard that *Morning Cloud* had been badly damaged in the gale, that five of the seven members of the crew had been washed ashore in a life-raft, but that two were still unaccounted for. A continuous search was being carried out for them. Later in the morning they confirmed that five of the crew were safe but in hospital. The two missing were my godson, Christopher Chadd, and Nigel Cumming. The police added that in the weather conditions still persisting on the south coast there was little hope that either could have survived. After telephoning Christopher's father with the terrible news, I drove down to the hospital where I was able to talk to the survivors, two of them badly injured, the rest still shocked by their experiences. They have since put together the whole story of the third *Morning Cloud's* last voyage.

When she sailed from Burnham on the Sunday morning, there had been a good breeze which had got up later in the day. After starting to take the inner channel along the Thames Estuary to Dover, the skipper decided to go about and take the outer one which would give him more room to manoeuvre. It was very rough going across to the North Foreland, but the boat went well and the crew were in good shape. The skipper did consider putting into Dover, but as conditions had somewhat improved he decided to carry on round the south coast. During the course of Monday, however, conditions got much worse, and late that night, while going round the Royal Sovereign light vessel, winds of 45–50 knots were recorded. At the same time, the seas were huge. The boat was down to a minimum of sail, with no headsail and the mainsail heavily reefed, but she was still doing 4–5 knots through the water. As there was a foul tide, she was making much less headway over the land.

When she was about six or seven miles from the Ower's light vessel, whose light was clearly seen by the skipper, *Morning Cloud* was hit by a large wave which threw her over on to her side. When she righted herself, the skipper found that one of the crewmen had gone overboard and was being held by his life-line. It took the crew several minutes in those conditions to haul him back on board. It was only then that they realized that another crewman had gone overboard, but his life-line had broken; the remnant was in the cockpit. They put *Morning Cloud* about to search for him, but to no avail. They resumed their course. The boat was then hit by a similar wave which also threw her on her side with the mast underwater. Once again, after what must have seemed to the crew an endless period, she righted herself. At the moment the second wave hit her, Christopher Chadd was just coming up the companion-way and he was swept overboard. He was wearing his lifejacket but he had not yet clipped on his life-line. In those tremendous seas the crew had one glimpse of him. That was all.

When the first wave knocked *Morning Cloud* on her side, some damage was done to the deck ribs of this stoutly-built boat. The second wave did more damage and the skipper found that she was carrying a lot of water. This had gone down the companion-way hatch and the forehatch, which had either been torn away by the wave or forced out by the pressure of air from the sudden inrush of water aft. Some of the water had been going in through other structural damage. The skipper decided that he would be unable to sail the boat in those conditions and launched the four-man life-raft. The top of the locker containing the six-man life-raft and the raft itself had been swept away by the waves. By an almost incredible feat the five remaining crew, including two who were by this time seriously injured – one had hurt his arm and ribs and the other his shoulder blade and ribs – clambered over the side into the raft, where they faced further difficulties. To most of them it seemed that their chances of survival were bleak. They let out the drogue to steady them in the water, and in those winds they had difficulties with the canopy over their heads. When they sent up their first flare, the wind was so strong that, although it went up, it was almost immediately blown down into the sea. Nobody on shore would have seen it. In the process two other flares packed with it got wet and would not go off at all.

This small life-raft was carried by wind and tide easterly along the coast and finally inshore. After escaping the danger of being thrown against Brighton Pier, the crew were faced with the likelihood of being smashed against the rocks piled up for the wall of the new marina. Before that was reached, however, they were tipped into the surf inshore. By a supreme effort they were able to cling on until the raft was washed on to the beach. The five men had survived for nearly eight hours in tempestuous seas. They owed their lives to that small life-raft.

It was a cruel blow that a boat built for heavy-weather sailing should have been destroyed in this way. As the coroner declared at the inquest, it was through no fault of the crew. At the time when the two large waves hit her, *Morning Cloud* was only a few miles from the protection of the Isle of Wight against the south-westerly gale. *Casse-Tête,* a forty-one-foot ocean-racing boat, rather smaller than *Morning Cloud,* which had been racing against her at Burnham throughout the previous week, made the same

voyage as *Morning Cloud* about an hour ahead of her. She got through safely, but her crew declared that those were the worst seas they had ever known.

There were lessons to be learnt from the tragedy. In particular, making the safety equipment more effective in such appalling conditions. The manufacturers have been provided with all the details of the way in which their equipment performed in this gale. However good the facilities for testing equipment may be, it is how it performs in the worst conditions experienced by sailors that matters. Although *Morning Cloud*'s equipment complied with all the safety requirements, in the gale of 2–3 September she was overwhelmed by the conditions at sea. We have already learnt the lesson about designing the cockpit so as to reduce the chances of a mass of water getting below. The danger of water in a storm affecting the engine and radio has been brought home to us again. We have increased the strength of our lifelines to double that of the safety requirements, and we have asked for the experiences of the crew in the life-raft to be taken into account by the manufacturers of the equipment inside it. Thus some good for all ocean sailors may come from the tragedy of the third *Morning Cloud*. In the same gale the first *Morning Cloud,* in which we had won the Sydney–Hobart Race, was torn from her moorings in Jersey and smashed against the rocks. The same sea and wind destroyed both.

I had not intended to have a new boat for the trials for the Admiral's Cup team in 1975. My original plan had been to make some changes in the third *Morning Cloud* so as to give her a better light-wind performance – to put more height on the mast and to give her extra sail area. Now I had to face the need for a new boat if I was to continue racing; but there was little time. The General Election in October and the new Parliament which followed took up all my time and energy for several months. It was not until towards the end of the year that I could give serious thought to the fourth *Morning Cloud* with Olin and Rod Stephens.

Boats for the 1975 races were already being built by the time Olin produced a design which he thought would meet our needs for an Admiral's Cup boat. Rod worked on the lay-out above and below deck with Owen Parker, who knew from our discussions as a crew where we wanted to develop the lay-out still further, based on our experiences of the third *Morning Cloud*. One major point was clear. There would be no time for the boat to be built in wood; it would have to be in aluminium alloy. I was sorry to leave Clare Lallow who had built so splendidly for us in the past. Again, this raised the question of finding a British builder who could produce a top-class ocean-racing boat in alloy. Fortunately, there were now two British firms whose experience of this had greatly increased since our decision two years previously to have another wooden boat. Olin produced designs by the middle of January, construction was immediately begun at Alldays in Gosport, the boat was finished off by Camper and Nicholson and

Below: The interior of the
fourth *Morning Cloud*.
The galley and (left) the
sleeping cots, more
comfortable than the bunks
we had previously

Right: Model of the fourth
Morning Cloud

launched on 10 May 1975; a total of four months from drawing
board to the water.

She is a beautiful boat, embodying all the latest in ocean-racing
equipment. Below she is, like all her predecessors, simple and
spartan. Arrangements for cots, which we now have instead of
bunks, are more comfortable than anything we have yet devised.
On deck we are flatter and cleaner than ever before, and the
working cockpit is shallower and more effective from the point of
view of handling the groups of winches. No doubt as time goes by
experience will show us further changes which can be made, but
this is as far as we can get at the moment.

The fourth *Morning Cloud* is a difficult boat to handle on the
wind. Reaching and running she is superb. On the wind she is
sensitive to changes to a degree none of us have previously
experienced. When everything is perfectly adjusted, we can get an
excellent performance from her. Perhaps the number of adjustments which can be made to so many different aspects of the boat
has produced complexities which are difficult to resolve. In any
case, we had all too short a time – just three weeks – to tune her
and master the art of sailing her for the Admiral's Cup trials.
On this occasion we did not gain the place that we earned in 1971
and 1973. Nor have we had the success this season which the three
previous *Morning Clouds* provided. Of the potential of the fourth
Morning Cloud I am, however, convinced.

Trials in the Solent 1975

Fourth *Morning Cloud* on trials in the Solent. Moving fast (previous pages) and (below) going to windward. It was hard work on the winches. Right: Richard Halpin, Terry Leahy, self, Owen Parker and Peter Nicholson, the navigator, gives a hand as well. Left: On the interlocking winch pedestal (left to right: Terry Leahy, Richard Halpin, David Carne). The fourth *Morning Cloud* is still more complicated than its predecessors. Owen Parker goes forward to see for himself (bottom right)

9 The Joys of Sailing and the Skills of Sailors

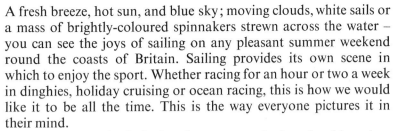

A fresh breeze, hot sun, and blue sky; moving clouds, white sails or a mass of brightly-coloured spinnakers strewn across the water – you can see the joys of sailing on any pleasant summer weekend round the coasts of Britain. Sailing provides its own scene in which to enjoy the sport. Whether racing for an hour or two a week in dinghies, holiday cruising or ocean racing, this is how we would like it to be all the time. This is the way everyone pictures it in their mind.

When the weather's foul and you are soaked to the skin, when there is low cloud and driving rain and visibility is almost nil, when the boat is being thrown around in a fierce sea, as, heavily reefed, she battles to windward; when down below it seems almost as wet as on deck and the heel of the boat makes cooking food in the galley a nightmare, then, certainly, you sometimes ask yourself why on earth you do it. Yet a fascination for sailing, and in particular for ocean racing, remains.

For those who sail dinghies, there is all the interest of a competitive sport. Today it is within the reach of young people all over the country, not only round the coast, but on inland waterways. They can band together to buy a boat and maintain it quite cheaply, they can join a club with good facilities at a modest subscription, and if they prove themselves successful they can trail their boat to other parts of the country for national and international contests. The helmsman of a dinghy is out there alone with his crew, the decisions rest on his judgement. On them depends success or failure. This breeds independence both of mind and spirit. At the same time, to get the boat going properly requires an almost instinctive understanding between two, or at the most three, people as they quickly adjust themselves to every change of the wind and tide, however slight, and at the same time cope with the tactics of getting into a race-winning position. On top of that there is the sheer physical excitement of being in a small boat moving at speed, often precariously balanced, with only a narrow margin between success and capsize. I found that small-boat sailing is a highly personal matter in which the skipper and his crew become more and more part of the boat, sensitive to its every need, feeling themselves a human extension of its material structure. There is no need to add that it is a healthy recreation. It both requires fitness and keeps you fit, it demands alertness and keeps you alert, and it provides its own satisfaction.

I can hardly speak for those who cruise for I have never done so myself. There has not been the time in a busy political life once racing has taken its toll of a few precious days of holiday. Moreover, each of the last three *Morning Clouds* has been designed and built as a racing machine. It would be difficult to cruise in them without a great deal of discomfort, though the fourth *Cloud* could easily be converted into an admirable fast-cruising boat. But I can recognize the enjoyment of living on a boat for a holiday, moving from place to place more or less as the spirit listeth, not pressed for time to round a mark or beat a competitor, and being able to find pleasure and relaxation in the beauty of our coastline with the hills behind it. For many, no doubt for all too brief a spell, it can be an almost timeless existence. Perhaps one day I may take up cruising.

Racing in larger boats, whether inshore or offshore, has a different attraction from that of dinghy racing, as I discovered when I changed over from one to the other. Of course it is just as competitive, perhaps even more so, and it can be just as thrilling. There is still the physical excitement, and, more than that, there is the intellectual excitement of being involved in the design and building of the boat, the organizational interest of running a complex machine, and the teamwork inseparable from handling a crew of ten determined to win if they possibly can. Ocean racing may lose some of the personal touch of one's hand on a dinghy tiller, but with it you move into a larger, more varied and even more interesting field.

I cannot deny that it is very demanding. The amount of thought and discussion which goes into the preliminary stage of the design and construction of a modern ocean-racing boat is immense. The organization required to keep the boat in tip-top condition for racing has to be highly specialized. Constant administrative arrangements are necessary to look after the requirements of the crew, including their food on board and their transport on shore. At sea there is the organization of watches, of helmsmen, of navigation, and the general running of the boat. In my experience the secret of success in all these is delegation to those who can take on individual responsibilities, but before you can delegate you must pick the right crew.

Picking the individuals for a crew and getting the right mix is an art in itself. The field for selection is somewhat limited by the comparatively small number of people who have the necessary skills and experience and who are also prepared to give up the time consistently to crewing. On alternate weekends in the summer offshore races begin on Friday evening and finish on Sunday. The crew must either be fortunate enough to be their own masters or able to persuade their employers to make the arrangements for them to have the necessary time off work. A wife or girlfriend may also have to be persuaded to acquiesce in this. I have always tried to help the crew of *Morning Cloud* by including wives and girlfriends in all our activities ashore, at home and abroad.

The best crew is a combination of many factors. Individual skill as a helmsman, navigator, winchman or foredeck hand is essential, combined with seamanship and a general ability to do at least one other job on the boat and preferably several. Sheer physical strength is a must in many cases: at the same time the greater the degree to which members of the crew have an intellectual appreciation of the basic principles of sailing, and their refinements, the better they will be able to cope with the continuous changes in boat design and sail development with which we are now faced. Specialist knowledge of particular items of equipment, sails, winches, electronics, and an ability to repair them, is invaluable. In its most highly developed form this specialist knowledge is usually the prerogative of those who work with the firms producing these items, and I have been fortunate that certain members of my crew have been associated with such firms. In addition to these technicians every top-class crew needs to contain some 'ideas men' – the two are not incompatible and when combined are a considerable force – to think through fresh solutions to old problems and to come forward with novel propositions, which can then be argued out, for making advances in the sport.

These individual skills are greatly influenced by the personality as well as the experience of the crewman. A helmsman may be most at home in light winds, sensitive to the merest puff, edging the boat along, never allowing it for a moment to stop. Another may be at his best in a blow, standing at the wheel in control for an hour or more against the elements which are battering both the boat and himself. A third may most enjoy steering her downwind, using the wave formation to give him just that extra bit of speed he needs to get ahead of his rivals. Whichever may be his métier, it demands an ability to hold the boat consistently on the edge of the wind or accurately on a compass course. When you add to that the advantage of being able to make a good start, of getting in amongst

Previous pages: The start of the 'Round the Goodwins' Race, August 1972. Below: Second *Morning Cloud* in her berth at Port Hamble, 1971. Left to right: Sammy Sampson, Duncan Kay, Peter Dove, Peter Holt, Anthony Churchill, Owen Parker, self

the other boats on the line, judging the most beneficial position for the course after allowing for wind and tide, finding a gap to get through and nipping into it, at the same time preventing yourself from being baulked by another boat, and midst it all keeping your nerve when surrounded by another sixty or so big boats from many different countries, then you have compiled a formidable job specification for the men who steer the boat. Ian Lallow, the son of the builder of the second and third *Morning Cloud*, undoubtedly one of the foremost helmsmen on the Solent, has met it to the full, both at home and in Australia. George Stead, who has had great success with his own one-tonner, is another. Sammy Sampson and Jean Berger, both from the East Coast, were among the first to steer with me. Owen Parker has done his share, knowing the Solent as well as anyone. On the fourth *Morning Cloud,* Peter Nicholson, whose firm was responsible for building the boat, has steered her beautifully as well as being navigator offshore.

The joys of sailing. Left: Hitting the mark! The Italian boat *Levantades* in the Admiral's Cup, 1971 Below: Third *Morning Cloud*'s spinnaker goes under the keel in the first short race in the Admiral's Cup, 1973. Not an example to follow!

To be a navigator today requires not only precision in dead reckoning – and an ability to insist on accurate reports from those steering the boat as a basis for it – but also a familiarity with the electronic aids we are allowed to use. The first is basic and too much reliance must not be placed on the latter. I suspect there are navigators who set a course and record their progress on it without worrying themselves unduly about it, relying on the fact that when they get near the mark they will be able to make whatever changes are necessary, however large, when they pick up their radio beacons. That is not good navigation and it is not the way to win races. The navigator also has to discover and allow for the characteristics of the boat in its performance in different weather conditions. The effect of tides is a common calculation – though I often doubt myself the reliability of tidal atlases – but how many make a

168

precise offset for the leeway of their boat on the wind? Over a leg of a hundred or a hundred and fifty miles a degree can make a considerable difference on the landfall. A navigator's life is not an enviable one, at beck and call on every watch, snatching sleep when he can, constantly having to choose between a variety of options, knowing full well that when successful he will receive little praise, but that if he makes a miscalculation the whole crew will rag him and damn him unmercifully. But then neither is life on the foredeck an easy one. Up on the bucking bow, changing down headsails in the dark in a storm, your harness hooked on to a lifeline, water sweeping over you, deafened by the noise of the waves and wind, demands guts and above all the ability to survive. Duncan Kay, who has been in the crew for six years, and Mark Dowland with him for the last four, form as tough and reliable a foredeck crew as one could wish for. Never for a moment do they hesitate, no matter what the conditions.

These individual skills and qualities are what I've sought to find in crewmen. To become an effective ocean-racing crew, more is needed from the crew as a whole – stamina, compatibility, the competitive spirit and courage. Don't jump to the conclusion that stamina means youth. I must confess it came as something of a surprise to me to discover that after a couple of days of watches four hours on and four hours off, younger people begin to flag, though there may be exceptions. It's only from the mid-twenties onward that endurance appears to become stabilized. It can then last well into the sixties, as Sir Francis Chichester showed us. Being prone to seasickness can be a problem. It's in no way blame-worthy, but it does reduce efficiency and taking tablets to quieten it also dulls the senses. Compatibility is another necessity – in building up a crew you have to find people who can get on with one another living for four or five days at sea in a cramped space in unpleasant, sometimes dangerous, conditions, tolerant of each other's foibles and mistakes, and prepared to lend each other a hand whenever opportunity offers. Some degree of tension may be unavoidable in the atmosphere of fierce competition which exists, but it must be containable.

To win requires competitive spirit to a high degree; to persist in the face of continued adversity even more. On *Morning Cloud* we have always raced to win. Over five years we have had more than our fair share of successes; when we have lost I hope we have done so with a good grace. Of course a sport must be kept in per-spective in the make-up of our lives. For the amateur – as we all are on the *Clouds* – it is recreation, a change, a contrast to our work, not something done in isolation but together as a team. In doing it our purpose is to win. Of course this is a contentious matter. There are some who believe that racing is an end in itself and that anything more involves the danger of professionalism. The latter is most unlikely. I have never paid anyone on a boat, and prize money on the scale of £5 for a win, £3 for a second and £1 for a third is hardly an inducement to participants to indulge in unsporting practices! To win is itself an incentive, and if by 'professionalism' is meant a professional or systematic approach to our sport and the challenges it poses, then I strongly believe in it. Without it we would never have made the progress we have done in these last few years and the rest of the world would have left us standing. Planning, preparation, operation, aiming always at perfection – these are just as important to the dinghy sailor in his local club as to the Olympic champion representing his country, as Rodney Pattisson has so often shown us; just as necessary to the boat doing a couple of courses inshore round the cans on a Saturday afternoon as to the ocean racer. I sometimes think that our form of racing, both inshore and offshore, is the most unfair of all sports. In a leading position you may fall into a calm which is certainly none of your making; those astern, seeing your predica-ment, sail out round you; the fleet leaves you behind. How often

Sailing needs stamina. Sir Francis Chichester (above) showed this to the full. He was photographed in *Gypsy Moth IV* some 400 miles from Plymouth and home (right), June 1968

COWESLIP

Far left: Two admired and famous sailors. Prince Philip, the Duke of Edinburgh (left), and Uffa Fox at Cowes

Lone round-the-world yachtsmen capture the imagination. Alec Rose (left) took part in the single-handed crossing of the Atlantic in 1964. Robin Knox-Johnston on *Suhaili* (bottom left) was a leading contender in the round-the-world non-stop race, 1969. Bottom right: He sits among his provisions

have I known this happen! Yet in a single race conditions may change so frequently, sometimes working to the advantage of the small boats, sometimes to the big, that the outcome is constantly in doubt. It is the will to win which always counts and that depends to a large extent on the morale of the crew.

On *Morning Cloud* we have tried as far as possible to do everything together as a crew. This begins with the discussions on the design and layout of the boat; it continues with an expression of views about new members of the crew. We have our own kit, in part for safety reasons, in part because it makes for unity. When away from home we dislike being broken up; we prefer to stay in the same place. After every race we like to be able to analyse it together – to try to learn from our mistakes – on the boat on its moorings if we cannot get together on shore. It is the constant exchange of views and information which binds a crew together and enables each of its members to act in the almost instinctive knowledge of what the others will do in any given situation. Of course this is an ideal, but it is worth taking time and trouble over. I was greatly helped in this when Owen Aisher kindly lent me his house in Cowes overlooking the Solent in 1970 and 1971. It was there that the crew met together for two years and the impact of our discussions on both the second *Morning Cloud* and the Admiral's Cup result was considerable. It has been more difficult since then to maintain the same level of communication, and the pressures on me of high office certainly made their contribution to the problem. I remain convinced that this is the only way to create a successful race-winning crew. No one has been more aware of this than Robin Aisher, captain of the British Admiral's Cup team in 1973 and again in 1975 when he led it to victory and regained the Admiral's Cup for Britain. He combines technical knowledge and skill with an openness of mind towards new ideas which has enabled him to skipper *Frigate* and *Yeoman XX* to successive triumphs in both inshore and offshore racing; whilst his will to win inspired not only his own crew but the whole British team.

What is it really like being on an ocean racer? I am constantly asked that question. I can only answer from my own experience of the four boats I have sailed. In a storm smaller boats than the first *Morning Cloud* must find life even more difficult than we did; no doubt bigger boats, from what I have seen on social occasions, have more room for their crews to stretch themselves. The tensions may be less as a result.

Technically, ocean racers are becoming more and more complex. Somewhat ironically the more the deck layout has been simplified and its components streamlined the more complicated have become the individual items of equipment and the adjustments to them. Earlier on I mentioned developments in winches. Sails provide another example. A mainsail today has seven major factors affecting it in operation: the cut of the sail itself, the rake of the mast, the position of the halyard, the tautness of the leech line,

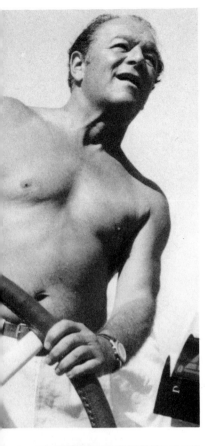

Top: Sir Max Aitken at the helm of *Crusade,* and (left) Robin Aisher steers *Frigate.* Above: Robin's father, Owen Aisher

the pull of the mainsheet, the position of the mainsheet traveller and the use of the flattener. In addition, the mainsail can be reefed when required. Each of these adjustments, with the exception of the cut of the sail, can be made at any time to suit any set of circumstances; indeed they have to be made as conditions vary, very often from one moment to the next. The problem is to get them all in the right place at the same time. This requires continuous concentration by the men on the helm and those trimming the sails.

Below deck on *Morning Cloud* priority is given to operational requirements; to the navigation section with its table, charts and instruments; to sail storage; to the galley; to the cots for sleeping; to the lockers for dry clothes and the zip bags for wet ones; and to the simple toilet and washbasin I have already described. There is no room for anything else. The routine is straightforward. We have two watches, each consisting of four members of the crew which do four hours on deck and then four hours below. If we have a major sail change to make or hit bad conditions we get the off-duty watch up to help. On long races one period for each watch is limited to two hours. This interrupts the sequence so that the same watch is not on duty for the same hours of the clock each day. The navigator and myself as skipper are not part of any watch. We are available at all times and snatch sleep when we can in quiet times. Once below, the off-duty watch, having taken off their wet oilskins and boots and put them ready to don quickly should they be called up suddenly, tend to roll into their cots to sleep. In rough weather they sleep in their clothes on top of the sleeping bags in case they have to leap out quickly, or otherwise stripped down and inside the bag. *Morning Cloud* carries only six cots, four for the watch off duty, with one for the navigator and one for myself. Exertions on deck, especially in heavy weather, and sail-packing below, particularly with frequent spinnaker-changing, means that sleep both comes naturally, even in the most difficult conditions, and is a high priority if the crew is to remain effective throughout a race. Tiredness brings mistakes and misjudgements. Pacing the crew both as individuals and as a unit is one of the keys to success. Another is feeding them well!

Someone has to work the galley and prepare the food. We are not large enough to carry a cook solely for that purpose. We have been lucky in always having members of each watch able to cook well, in addition to their other duties. A full breakfast of orange juice, eggs, bacon, sausages, mushrooms and toast is what the crew of *Morning Cloud* like – and nowhere does it taste better than early on a clear summer morning at sea. We go for fresh meat, steaks and chops, with canned or dried vegetables for the hot meals for the first two or three days of a race, kept fresh in the icebox with large blocks of ice in the bottom, and precooked food, chicken or cutlets with salads for the cold midday meal. It depends on the cook's skill and habits as to whether he adds his own pet fancies

to the meal from whatever he finds in packages and tins. In an attempt to treat the feeding of the crew scientifically I once organized a tasting of the various brands of tinned and packaged food: it is important the crew should like what they eat and at the same time helpful to limit the extra weight brought on board. We were all surprised at the differences we found existed between the different brands. It was a revealing experience. We made our choice and have stuck to it. Our approach to the equipment in the galley is similarly functional so that it can be handled with the minimum expenditure of effort even in bad conditions. Papier-mâché plates and cups which can afterwards be thrown overboard save the washing-up, but someone still has to cope with knives and forks, pots and pans. No one likes it and nothing on board causes more irritation than for one watch to find that the previous one has left it the washing-up to do.

Some would say it is a simple life – away from it all. It can be, if you ignore the radio on board – and we don't carry a cassette player. It is certainly varied, at times physically exacting and mentally demanding, at others frustrating to the point of extreme boredom. There is an element of danger inseparable from the sport, whether from overstrained equipment on board or from other ships, especially when crossing traffic lanes in fog. The perils of the sea also help to bind a crew together, for every member of it knows that his life, like theirs, depends on their joint efforts. Is there ever fear at sea? Yes, of course. No one who has taken part in ocean racing would want to deny that; but action is often an effective antidote to fear and the need for action is seldom lacking in bad conditions at sea. And sometimes there is personal grief at the loss of a fellow sailor and, very rarely, at the loss of a boat. The sea always demands respect.

The crew of each *Morning Cloud* has been under additional strains not shared by other crews, above all that of the continuing and probably inescapable publicity to which the boats have been subjected. Any mistake in tactics, any mishandling of the boat, any minor mishap such as going aground – which we did at the entrance to Ramsgate harbour as a result of the Admiralty chart not yet having been corrected – which would pass unnoticed with any other boat, at once become front page news for *Morning Cloud*. To start the Fastnet Race in 1971 and again in 1973 with the high-pitched screech of three helicopters directly overhead following us down the Solent, accompanied by six or eight launches of press reporters and photographers, stretched the nerves to the utmost. The crew has stood it well.

Sailing has given me the opportunity of getting to know those whom I would not otherwise have met. One of the joys has been to share their interests, not on the basis of politics or business, but solely on the merits of what we have been trying to achieve in our own chosen field. They have shown me kindness and understanding.

The Royal Ocean Racing Club readily accepted me as a newcomer and within two years I had been made captain of the British Admiral's Cup team. I have made it a rule never to play any part in sailing politics – or musical politics for that matter; ordinary politics are quite enough for one life! Commodore of the House of Commons Yacht Club – a purely nominal post – is the only flag office I have held. It is natural that some boats and crews always seem to be able to get on with each other; some don't. With our connections our relations have been particularly close and enjoyable with the Australians, the Americans and the New Zealanders in international contests, and with the Irish, who regularly come to Cowes. Strangely enough our European contacts are fewer in number. A lasting and somewhat special relationship exists between us and other boats which have been in the British team. It is with their skippers, Arthur Slater of *Prospect of Whitby,* Bob Watson of *Cervantes,* Donald Parr of *Quailo,* John Prentice of *Battlecry,* Ron Amey of *Noryema,* and Robin Aisher the last team captain, that I have worked most closely. Bob Watson's goblet, engraved to celebrate our 1971 victory in the Admiral's Cup, adorns my house today.

It is sometimes said that sailing is just a rich man's sport. In fact it is no different from the great majority of activities in our daily lives. There is a place for everyone, from the small dinghy sailor to the large yacht owner. On each weekend in Britain from April to September there are over two million people messing around in boats of one kind or another, enjoying a healthy active recreation – more than spend their time watching football each winter Saturday, not participators, just spectators. What is more important than the sort of boat you have or what it costs you is the fact that sailing and, in particular, racing is a classless sport. A typical crew contains people from widely varying backgrounds and differing individual circumstances. What they are is of no importance to their colleagues: it is what they do as members of the crew that matters. This attitude of mind must surely be valuable in other spheres in our society today and deserves to be encouraged.

In Britain we have been fortunate in the support we have been given and the example we have been set by our leading yachtsmen. Owen Aisher has constantly stimulated activity in the sailing world, not only by his own achievements, including winning the Fastnet Race in 1951 in *Yeoman III* – at the age of seventy-five he has now reached *Yeoman XX* – but also by his attention to administration. In moments of disappointment he has constantly urged me on – with a vigorous philosophy determined to overcome all difficulties. The personal triumphs of Max Aitken in a long line of famous boats have been even more varied, but with them he has combined many other activities. His support for the annual Boat Show in London has been invaluable both to the boatbuilding industry and to all those interested in boats, whether they own

Opposite: The contrasts of sailing. Above: Action. Shouting at the foredeck, third *Morning Cloud,* 1971. Below: Frustration – no wind at all, and time for an apple. Fourth *Morning Cloud,* Cowes Week, 1975

one or not. It was there that I was proud to receive from his hands the Yachtsman of the Year Award for 1970, elected by the yachting correspondents. I gently chided him afterwards saying that at the end of the year, when I handed it back, there would be nothing to show for it. He took the hint. Since then a replica, to be retained, has been provided – I have the first. But perhaps many will remember most the splendid hospitality he has so often provided for visiting boats, particularly from the Commonwealth and the United States, in that glorious converted sail loft overlooking the Medina River at Cowes, which contains so many historic treasures connected with sailing. These first aroused my interest in models of ships, of which I now have a number of *Morning Cloud* as well as others made by French prisoners-of-war during the Napoleonic period.

Those sailors who have circumnavigated the globe in modern times have written their own stories. Alec Rose comes from my part of the world, East Kent. Born in Canterbury, in business in Ramsgate, he launched his first boat at Broadstairs – we have that in common, and he has always shown great interest in *Morning Cloud*. But then he has never spared himself in giving freely of his wisdom and experience to sailors all over the country. Robin Knox-Johnston's family also live in Kent, rather nearer my constituency than my home. This connection was one of the reasons why I agreed to take part in a television interview with him after his return from his single-handed voyage, though I knew how little experience I had in comparison with his. I was intrigued to find out whether he had been affected at all by his long period alone at sea. By way of starting the programme the interviewer said, 'I'm sure that what our listeners would like to hear, Mr Knox-Johnston, is what you missed most during your long lone voyage.' Without a moment's hesitation Robin replied, 'Well, you know what I missed most, but I also missed good food and wine.' I thought to myself that anyone who could come back instantly with that retort certainly hadn't lost touch with reality.

With Francis Chichester and his wife Sheila I shared a love of music as well as sailing, and together we discussed the technicalities of stereo reproduction when he was presented with a set after his historic voyage. It was that voyage which focused the eyes of the British people once again on the sea. I shall always remember his landing at Plymouth on his return home. Like millions of others I watched it on television. There was first the disappointing announcement that because there was so little wind he was unlikely to make the Hoe by nightfall. Then, as dusk fell, *Gypsy Moth* appeared and he stepped ashore. What a moving moment that was. Then came the press conference. Francis Chichester was halting, parrying, stumbling – how I felt for him! Finally a young journalist asked him the question for which somehow everyone was waiting: 'Sir Francis, why did you do it?' Straightaway his eyes lit up and without pausing came the answer: 'Because it intensifies life.'

Because it intensifies life!

For me, like many others, sailing provides a recreation which stretches me physically and intellectually in another direction from my daily life in politics. When I return to the fray I do so refreshed, ready to see the ever-recurring problems in a new light. It is important for a politician to retain as fully as he can such a creative activity, even though politics in general and government in particular must always take first priority. When I held the talks with President Pompidou in Paris in May 1971 which led to the successful conclusion of the negotiations for Britain's entry into the European Community, we had both planned that the meeting would end with the lunch which the French President would attend at the British Embassy on the second day, a Friday. I was then to fly home, travel down to *Morning Cloud* and sail in the Channel Race that evening. At lunchtime we found we could make much greater progress than we had expected; we decided to carry on with the talks. My private secretary sent a message to *Morning Cloud* to sail on without me. That evening, when all had been settled, President Pompidou said to me, 'Well, you have missed your race. A fortnight ago you won. What do you want to happen this time? Is it better for them to win without you, in which case it will show you don't matter, or not to win, in which case *Morning Cloud* has lost an important race just before your Admiral's Cup trials? Which is it to be?' There was nothing I could do either way. *Morning Cloud* settled it by coming second!

Because it intensifies life!

There are moments of intense beauty at sea, often unexpected. It is not only the colour, the life, the gaiety of the unforgettable Cowes Week of 1975, perfect in every way except for the lack of wind on almost every day. It is not only the peace of eventide as the sun sets over the moorings at Burnham when the first touches of autumn appear. There is the beauty of the sea itself. Of all these scenes, the one which remains clearest in my mind was in the early morning of the last day of the Fastnet Race in August 1973. On deck, almost becalmed, I watched the sun gently rising through the low haze. Suddenly I realized I was seeing in colour for the first time what the Impressionists and those who followed them had seen. Between *Morning Cloud* and the sun the rippling sea was a multicoloured patchwork of brilliant yellows, purples and greens, all dancing together. My mind leapt to Derain: he had just such a vision; he was able to convey it to others in paint. On the other side of *Morning Cloud,* out of the sun, everything was a smooth Whistlerian grey.

Because it intensifies life!!

Perhaps we have been able to make some impact on the development of sailing, and of ocean racing in particular, in Britain over these last few years. I believe it to be so and I hope it will be a permanent contribution to the sport.

Above all, I would like to think that to many people, and especially to young people, we have been able to convey through *Morning Cloud* something of a philosophy of life: that refreshment of body and mind, in whichever way appeals, is an essential element in a full life; that it is not longer hours of harder, drearier work that are needed to solve our problems, either personal or national, but a more effective effort to attain the highest standards to which we can aspire; that this is something we can do together, regardless of background or status, class or creed; that what the future holds for us depends on what we choose to make of our opportunities. The pursuit of excellence should be our purpose; its achievement brings its own satisfaction. If we have been able to convey these thoughts, however inadequately, however indirectly, to some of our fellow countrymen, I shall be well content.

3 September 1975

Below: Coming ashore at the end of Burnham Week, having won every race. Second *Morning Cloud*, 1972. Left to right: Self, Owen Parker, at the rear Anthony Churchill

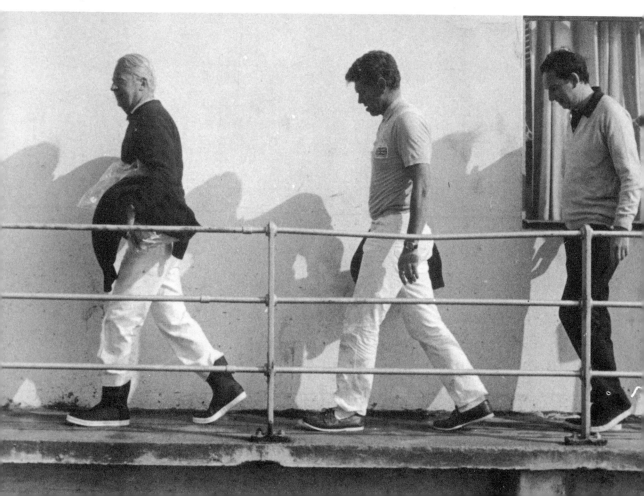

Edward Heath: Sailing Biography

1965	**Edward Heath elected Leader of the Conservative Party, the Opposition party**
1966	
Summer	EH decides to take up sailing on a Foreland class (18-foot)
1967	EH buys Snipe class, *Blue Heather* (16-foot)
1968	
January	EH buys Fireball, *Blue Heather II* (just over 16-foot)
1969	
January	EH buys S&S 34, first *Morning Cloud* (nearly 34-foot, Sparkman & Stephens design)
April	*Morning Cloud* launched
August	Wins the Ramsgate Gold Cup
December	Southern Cross series in Australia *Morning Cloud* selected as reserve boat in the British team
30 December	*Morning Cloud* wins the Sydney–Hobart Race
1970	**Conservatives win the General Election**
June	**Edward Heath becomes Prime Minister**
August	*Morning Cloud* wins the Commodore's Cup at Burnham
1971	
Easter	Second *Morning Cloud* launched (40-foot, Sparkman & Stephens design, built by Clare Lallow)
July	*Morning Cloud* chosen for British team for Admiral's Cup EH captain of the team *Morning Cloud* wins the 'Round the Island' Race, Cowes Week
August	Admiral's Cup, won by Britain
December	*Morning Cloud* wins her class in the Sydney–Hobart Race (EH not on board)
1972	
August	*Morning Cloud* wins the 'Round the Island' Race for the second successive year *Morning Cloud* wins the Town Cup, Burnham Week
1973	
April	Third *Morning Cloud* launched (45-foot, Sparkman & Stephens design, built by Clare Lallow) *Morning Cloud* selected for British team for Admiral's Cup
July	*Morning Cloud* wins the 'Round the Island' Race for the third successive year
1974	
February	**Conservative Party loses the General Election** **Edward Heath becomes Leader of the Opposition**
August	Cowes Week. *Morning Cloud* wins the New York Yacht Club Cup Ramsgate. *Morning Cloud* wins the 'Round the Goodwins' Race
3 September	*Morning Cloud* badly damaged in gale while being taken back to Cowes by 'movement crew' and sank at sea. Two members of the crew lost —continued overleaf

October	General Election won by the Labour Party
1975	
February	Edward Heath relinquishes Leadership of the Conservative Party
May	Fourth *Morning Cloud* launched (45-foot, Sparkman & Stephens design, built by Alldays in Gosport and Camper and Nicholson)
August	Cowes Week. *Morning Cloud* participates
	Burnham Week. *Morning Cloud* wins on points

Sailing Events in which *Morning Cloud* Competed

'Round the Island' Race (from Cowes, round the Isle of Wight and back to Cowes. 60 miles. Founded 1931. Award: Gold Roman Bowl)	July
Cowes–Dinard Race (date varies each year, but usually July. Approximately 180 miles. 9 prizes, including tankards, cups, etc.)	July
Pattinson Cup (Mersea to Burnham. 53 miles. Founded 1948)	August
ADMIRAL'S CUP (founded 1957, and takes place in '*Cowes Week*', an event already established in the sailing calendar. There are four races, see below)	August
Channel Race (from Cowes, the course only being decided 10 minutes before the start of the race. 220 miles)	
Two 30-mile races round the Solent: Royal Ocean Racing Club Race Royal Yacht Racing Club Race	
Fastnet Race (Cowes to Fastnet Rock in Ireland, ending in Plymouth. 605 miles)	
'Round the Goodwins' Race, Ramsgate (founded 1959. 55 miles. Noot Cup)	
'*Burnham Week*' (founded 1892; courses are decided daily)	August/September
Town Cup Race	
Commodore's Cup Race	
Burnham Trophy	
SOUTHERN CROSS CUP SERIES, Australia	December
One 220-mile ocean race	
Two 30-mile races	
Sydney–Hobart Race	

Index

Photo acknowledgements

Associated Press 66; Australian Information Service 9, 11, 63, 68; Chris Barham 167; Beken of Cowes 3, 80, 122, 127; John Bethell 17, 30t. 71, 83, 97-98, 101-102, 109, 138, 139, 176; Alistair Black 4, 72tl, 100tl, 103-104, 105, 160-161, 162t, 162b, 163t, 163b; J. Allan Cash 36; Central Press 120; Gerry Cranham 88-89, 132-133, Daily Telegraph 74-75, 140, 182, 186-7; Financial Times 116; Paul Forrester 107-8, 159; Barry Fountain 81; Fox Photos 22; 77b, 87, 100b; Ambrose Greenaway 44-45, 46, 48, 169, 174t, 174b; Keystone Press Agency 39, 40, 171, 175b; Life Editorial Services 72, 96, 130, 131, 136-7; London Express 30b, 115, 136, 156; London Express/David Cairns 2, 148-9, 150, 151, 152, 158, 178b; Brian Manby 86, 93, 106; Photo Patrol, Sydney 82; Popperphoto 172b, 173t; Peter Powell 14, 19, 22, 23, 24-25, 26, 27, 29, 111; Press Association 12lt; Qantas 52-3, 56, 59, 60-61; Laurie Richards 118, 119; Roger Smith 42-43, 84-5, 90-91, 92, 99t, 99b, 100tr; Sport and General 37, 128; Sports Illustrated 124, 144, 168; Syndication International 172t, 173b; Captain Tom Taylor RM 135; Topix 35, 178t; Chris Wood 112; Yachting Photo-Jean Dupuy 95

Overleaf: Second *Morning Cloud* at Burnham 1972